Enhancing Prim

C000076649

Enhancing Primary Science

Developing Effective
Cross-Curricular Links

Edited by

Lois Kelly and Di Stead

Mc
Graw
Hill   Open University Press

Open University Press
McGraw-Hill Education
McGraw-Hill House
Shoppenhangers Road
Maidenhead
Berkshire
England
SL6 2QL

email: enquiries@openup.co.uk
world wide web: www.openup.co.uk

and Two Penn Plaza, New York, NY 10121-2289, USA

First published 2013

A catalogue record of this book is available from the British Library

ISBN-13: 9780335247042 (pb)
ISBN-10: 0335247040 (pb)
e-ISBN: 9780335247059

Library of Congress Cataloging-in-Publication Data
CIP data has been applied for

Typeset by Aptara Inc., India
Printed and bound by CPI Group (UK) Ltd, Croydon, CR0 4YY

The McGraw·Hill Companies

Praise for this book

"Let this book take you by the hand and guide you skilfully past the pitfalls of cross-curricular teaching in primary science whilst enjoying the celebration of creative and effective links between science and other subjects. It is full of practical suggestions for cross-curricular work but it never loses sight of the need for clear learning goals. Rooted in the principles of collaborative learning, this book inspires and informs."

Anne Goldsworthy, Independent Science Consultant

"This important book explores a practical framework for cross curricular teaching of science through a closely referenced theoretical rationale. There are a range of open ended tasks that illustrate the rich learning opportunities that can be planned for when expert subject knowledge combines with a pedagogy for enquiry. This is an essential read for all teachers inspired to tailor the curriculum to the needs and interests of their children."

Alison Peacock, Head Teacher of The Wroxham School and Transformative Learning Alliance, Network Leader for the Cambridge Primary Review

"I enjoyed this book sharing insights into cross curricular approaches to primary science. The authors have successfully demonstrated how they have put theory into practice. There are many useful activities clearly outlined for use in the classroom based on the authors own experiences. The reader will gain sound knowledge and understanding of how and why cross curricular approaches can enhance primary science through worked examples. My particular favourite was the History of Bread. I will certainly recommend this book to my students."

Kathy Schofield, Senior Lecturer for Primary Science, Manchester Metropolitan University, UK

Contents

List of figures

List of tables

Notes on contributors

Alison Brade is a Senior Lecturer in Primary English in Education at Liverpool Hope University. She taught for several years in the primary sector and during this time, at different stages, she was subject leader for English, assessment, design and technology (D&T) and information and communications technology (ICT). She then became an advisory teacher supporting teachers at all phases in all aspects of the teaching of English. She has carried out research into cross-curricular writing and has regularly worked with specialists in other subjects to develop children's reading and writing across the curriculum. She has a keen interest in children's literature, particularly how it supports children's development in reading and writing, and is researching this as part of her doctoral studies.

Mark Hamill is a freelance trainer, researcher and educational consultant. He was a teacher educator for over a decade. Prior to this, he was an advisory teacher for Religious Education in the North West of England. Mark trained as a primary teacher but has taught students of all ages. His research interests lie in the interplay between theology and education, especially in the context of academies and free schools.

Sharon Harris is a Senior Lecturer in the School of Education at the University of Brighton, where she teaches primary science on both PGCE and BA (Hons) routes. She taught in primary, middle and British International schools for 20 years, coordinating science in six of them. She worked as Primary Science Advisor for Northamptonshire Inspection and Advisory Service (NIAS) for four years and was also a Team Inspector for Ofsted with a remit for primary science. She has become increasingly interested in the potential for linking science with the arts, having always had a passion for music, photography and painting. Working with Alison Hermon, she established an optional Year 3 module on the BA (Hons), 'SciArt – Creative Collaborations', to explore these links. Through this they developed a partnership with the Wakehurst Place annual 'Big Draw' event in October. She has been a member of the Association for Science Education (ASE) since 1988.

Shelagh Hendry has taught all age groups at primary level in Oldham and Manchester schools since 1993. Most recently she has been Senior Primary Consultant for Oldham Council responsible for mathematics, science and Year 6. In this role, she provided support for primary teachers, newly and recently qualified teachers (NQTs and RQTs) in both science and mathematics. She has held regular network meetings for science subject leaders and supported a project linking primary and secondary science teaching to increase effective progression. She is presently delivering the local authority element of the Mathematics Specialist Teacher programme for Oldham teachers under the auspices of Manchester Metropolitan University and Liverpool Hope University. She is co-author of *Numbers and Patterns*, a National Strategy document (2009), supporting mathematics at the transition from EYFS to Key Stage 1. She is a member of the Association of Teachers of Mathematics, the National Advisers and Inspectors Group for Science, and the Association for Science Education.

Alison Hermon is a Senior Lecturer in the School of Education at the University of Brighton, teaching art and design on the BA (Hons) Primary, and both primary and secondary PGCE courses. At the same time she has been engaged in her own creative practice as a sculptor and maker. The materials and methods she uses in her own artwork have a strong scientific component, and therefore establishing a cross-curricular optional module, 'SciArt – Creative Collaborations', gave her an opportunity to share these passions with students. On an international level, since the beginning of 2010 she has designed and developed an Art and Design curriculum for primary and secondary schools in partnership with the University of Cambridge and the Egyptian government. She has taught all age groups across the primary and secondary phases. She has contributed to a number of publications on the subject of art and design and special educational needs and disability (SEND).

Pat Hughes was a Senior Lecturer at Liverpool Hope University for 20 years, where she taught history and professional studies to primary PGCE students. She has published widely with Fulton, Scholastic, Oxford University Press, Heinemann, Nelson, Hopscotch, Folens, Multi-lingual Matters, and Paul Chapman.

Arthur Kelly is a Senior Lecturer in Education at Liverpool Hope University, where he is curriculum leader for primary geography working on undergraduate and PGCE courses. He has also led modules on primary science in initial teacher education (ITE). His undergraduate degree in geography included elements of physical geography, including geology and meteorology. He taught for 14 years in the primary sector and during this time, at different stages, he was subject leader for geography, environmental education, science and physical education. The taught elements of his masters degree focused on primary science pedagogy. He has a keen interest in children's learning, particularly geographical learning, and has spoken and published at a national and international level on this subject. He is a moderator for the Primary Geography Quality Mark, a national scheme benchmarking standards in primary geography; a member of the editorial board for *Primary Geography* and a Geography Champion. His doctoral studies focus on children's geographies and their understandings of the world.

Lois Kelly is a teacher educator and education consultant. She has provided primary science continuing professional development (CPD) in the North West of England, the Isle of Man and internationally. She worked in ITE for ten years at Liverpool Hope University where she was Curriculum Coordinator for Primary Science on BA (QTS) and PGCE courses. Prior to this she taught for 20 years in both primary and middle schools, during which time she taught across the primary age range and was, at different times, mathematics coordinator and science subject leader. Before the advent of the Qualifications and Curriculum Authority (QCA) schemes of work, the Literacy Strategy and the Numeracy Strategy, she was responsible for developing the curriculum in her school using thematic, cross-curricular themes. Recently she worked with colleagues to develop modules to enable students to explore cross-curricular approaches to teaching and learning. Lois contributed to Christine Bold's *Supporting Learning and Teaching* in 2011 (published by Routledge). She is a member of the Primary Committee of the Association for Science Education and has presented workshops at ASE events promoting cross-curricular approaches in science education. She is a hub leader for the Primary Science Quality Mark.

Liz Lawrence has been Advisory Teacher for Primary Science and Technology in the London Borough of Barking and Dagenham since 1999. Before that she taught for 14 years in primary schools in North East London and Essex. She has experience of coordinating music, science, C and D&T, and of senior leadership. She served for ten years on the Association for Science Education's Primary Science Committee, five of them as Chair, and has been elected as Chair of the Association for 2012–13. She was part of the expert group writing the scientific and technological understanding area of learning for the New Primary Curriculum (published February

2010 but not implemented). Her involvement in science and D&T links also includes membership of the original working group planning a science and D&T course for the Science Learning Centres and a joint project between ASE and the Design and Technology Association, of which she is a member, developing project ideas to exemplify effective linking of the two subjects. As part of this, she presented workshops at ASE and Design and Technology Association events. She has written for ASE on the subjects of health and safety, subject leadership and scientific enquiry. She is a Chartered Science Teacher.

Cliff Porter writes science education materials for publication and web-based resources. In addition, he delivers training to teachers and classroom assistants on a variety of topics including the use of ICT to enhance teaching and learning in science. Prior to becoming a full-time education consultant, Cliff taught for 12 years in secondary schools, a tertiary college, and finally as a university lecturer delivering science courses to trainee primary teachers. A sample of the education materials he has developed include: 'Enhancing Science with ICT' courses at the National Science Learning Centre and North West Regional Centre and ASE 'Getting Practical' courses for primary teachers. He has edited and developed resources for Channel 4 Clipbank, Primary Science Enhancement Programme and web-based resources for the Schoolscience website. He co-authored 'Learning to Love Science', a research project for Shell Education Services, and reported on the establishment of the UK Space Education Resource Office for the European Space Agency.

Di Stead is an educational consultant, working with primary teachers and their schools. She has provided science in-service training from the north of England to India. She worked for almost two decades in higher education, at Liverpool Hope University for over 17 years and before that at Bishop Grosseteste College in Lincoln. Working with colleagues Tim Griffiths and Pat Hughes, she produced two DVDs, 'Earth and Beyond' and 'Science Games', which include practical ideas for teaching science. Before working in initial teacher education, Di worked as a BP fellow at the Chemical Industry Education Centre (CEIC) at the University of York, writing curriculum materials. During this time she learned the importance of providing interesting and everyday contexts for learning science. She has maintained links with CIEC and an interest in industry–education links. She learned her craft teaching in a primary school in the East End of Sheffield for 14 years. Her first publication, *CLUES: Science in a Topic*, in 1984 with Robin Smith of Sheffield Hallam University and a teaching colleague Janet Wilkinson, looked at teaching science in a cross-curricular way. She renewed this interest in cross-curricular teaching more recently through her teaching on initial teacher education courses.

Acknowledgements

We would like to thank the following for their contributions to this book, whose help and enthusiasm have brought the book alive:

The staff and children at St Elizabeth's RC Primary School, Litherland, Merseyside.

The staff and children at St George's CE Primary School, Stockport.

Carol Williams, Headteacher at Hursthead Junior School, Cheadle Hulme.

Figures 2.1, 2.2, 2.3, 2.4, 5.2, 5.3, 6.1, 6.2, 6.4, 6.5, 6.6, 11.1b, 11.2, 11.3, 11.4, 11.5, cover image reproduced with thanks to Di Stead and copyright reserved.

Figures 4.1, 4.2, 4.3, 4.4, 4.5 reproduced with thanks to Cliff Porter and copyright reserved.

Figure 5.1 reproduced with thanks to Arthur Kelly and copyright reserved.

Figures 8.1, 8.2, 8.3, 8.4, 8.5 reproduced with thanks to Sharon Harris and Alison Hermon and copyright reserved.

Figures 9.1, 9.4, 9.5 reproduced with thanks to Millgate House Publishing and copyright reserved.

Figures 9.2, 9.3 reproduced with thanks to Liz Lawrence and copyright reserved.

Figure 10.1 and Tables 10.1, 10.2 reproduced with thanks to Hursthead Junior School and copyright reserved.

Preface

I am old enough to have been a 'child of Clegg' and to have planned and taught an integrated curriculum as a young teacher.

I was educated in Yorkshire at the time when Sir Alec Clegg, a forward-looking educationalist, was Chief Education Officer of Yorkshire County Council West Riding. In my primary school I worked on a table with a group of my peers, where I was encouraged to explore, speculate and offer my own ideas. The much quoted phrase that we need to

> supply the pupils with what is essential for their healthy growth, physical, intellectual and moral ... and that the curriculum is to be thought of in terms of activity and experience rather than of knowledge to be acquired and facts to be stored

emphasized by the 'The Primary School' consultative committee report in 1931 (Galton et al., 1980) described my own primary school education.

Subsequently I trained at a college which encouraged us to think about a child-centred approach to teaching and learning rather than a subject-centred approach. Plowden (CACE, 1967) was often cited as a reason for educating the whole child, socially and emotionally. I learned the significance of this emphasis on educating children socially and emotionally when I started teaching in the East End of Sheffield, in the late 1970s and early 1980s.

The school I taught in offered a greater focus on a skills-based curriculum than a knowledge-based curriculum. As science coordinator, I supported my colleagues to encourage the use of scientific enquiry skills. What the children found out did not seem to be as important as how they found out and whether they could trust their findings. At the same time, as a school we embraced what Maurice Galton was promoting: that cooperative group work not only extended social skills but also enhanced cognitive outcomes. However, later on in the mid-1980s, I remember my headteacher at the time asking me what scientific knowledge I would like the children to know before they left the primary school for secondary school. This was all before the National Curriculum.

My first publication was *CLUES: Science in an Integrated Topic* (Smith et al., 1984). It was 1984 and Robin Smith from Sheffield Hallam University was a participant observer in a forensic science topic in our school. The school was open plan, the teachers planned cooperatively and team taught. Teachers also used their expertise to plan learning for a larger number of children and to support colleagues. Rotational group work was employed to make good use of teachers' time, by planning a balance between teacher-intensive activities and self-sustaining activity. The focus of the topic was a crime scene. A burglary was staged: a valuable coin collection being used as a sorting activity went missing. Throughout the day a number of visitors/suspects such as a plumber and a window cleaner came into the open plan unit, leaving clues. The children were taking part in a real life drama and tried to make sense of what had happened. They looked for evidence, for example exploring the ink in pens each suspect left behind. Their enquiry was not compartmentalized into subject areas. Although science-based, it was easy to make links with other curriculum areas. For example, with the help of the community police officer children wrote witness statements.

I had been taught to make use of a spider diagram, a technique rather like mind mapping as a method for medium-term planning. This enabled us not only to look at discrete subject areas but also make links between them. The skill of the teacher was to plan activities so that the children could use ideas and skills learned in one activity and build on them in the next planned activity. These links enriched and enhanced their learning. However the real skill was knowing when *not* to make links in the planning. We were aware that making tenuous links between subjects was the downfall of this approach. I did hear horror stories of what was happening in other schools, perhaps where staff had not seen the benefits to learning of this approach. Links were being made that were so tenuous they did not complement the learning. Judith Laurie uses the example of including *Come Away from the Water, Shirley* by John Burningham in a topic of 'water' (Burningham, 1992; Laurie, 2011: 128).

Criticism of a curriculum which overemphasized cross-curricular topic work was reinforced by the work done in the late 1980s in Leeds by Robin Alexander (reported in 1992). In 1985 Leeds City Council introduced a five-year project, the 'Primary Needs Programme', which Alexander evaluated. His findings were published in 1989. Leeds City Council envisaged an ambitious (some said an overambitious) model of good practice. One of its elements included children working on different areas of the curriculum at the same time. One of the findings from the evaluation – the lack of observed improvements – was ambushed by the press at the time to show that this kind of progressive education was not effective (Galton et al., 1999).

Later, Alexander, along with Sir Jim Rose and Chris Woodhead (1992), in what was known as the 'Three Wise Men' report, went on to say:

> There is clear evidence to show that much topic work has led to fragmentary and superficial teaching and learning. There is also ample evidence to show that teaching focused on single subjects benefits primary pupils. We see a need both for more sharply-focused and rigorously-planned topic work and for an increase in single subject teaching.
>
> (Alexander et al., 1992: para 3.4)

The new National Curriculum (DfES, 1989; DfEE/QCA, 1999) was based on curriculum entitlement rather than dictating teaching methods and teaching styles. It made a broad and balanced curriculum the entitlement of each child and was organized into separate subjects, rather than being skill-based or based around broad concept areas which may have cut across subjects, as some as us had hoped. The gossip around at the time was that planning the National Curriculum was left to subject committees and colleagues in secondary and tertiary education. Getting my head around the new curriculum was paramount, and resulted in planning to teach the separate subjects as set out in the new curriculum. The curriculum felt overloaded. Finding links between the subject documents seemed too difficult in the first instance so we didn't do it.

Over the years we looked on at our colleagues in the Foundation Stage and Early Years and marvelled at their approach. I always thought that we have a lot to learn from them.

It seems that we have come full circle, with a renewed interest in cross-curricular working in primary schools.

Conclusion

We must learn from history and make sure we do not repeat the mistakes of Leeds City Council in the 1980s and enforce a cross-curricular way of working on every teacher in every school. I am sure that it is not envisaged that everyone will adopt one approach all the time, or that if a school is not at the point to explore a cross-curricular approach then they should not proceed. When cross-curricular teaching is not fit for purpose then separate subject teaching should be employed and teachers should trust their professional judgement.

The purpose of this book is to offer those schools and teachers who want to adopt a cross-curricular approach a pragmatic view of how to successfully embark on this method of teaching and learning. We hope that there is a balance between thinking about teaching in a cross-curricular way and plenty of ideas of how to put the advice into practice.

We have provided a rationale for teaching science in a cross-curricular way, considering the benefits and challenges of this approach. The bulk of the book includes some suggestions of how to make links between science and other areas of the curriculum and some reminders about planning. We hope that the voices of the children and teachers who helped us enrich this book speak through about teaching and learning in a cross-curricular way. Happy teaching!

Di Stead

References

Alexander, R.J., Rose, A.J. and Woodhead, C. (1992) *Curriculum Organisation and Classroom Practice in Primary schools: A Discussion Paper*. London: Department of Education and Science.

Burningham, J. (1992) *Come Away from the Water, Shirley*. London: Red Fox.

Central Advisory Council for Education (CACE) (1967) *Children and their Primary Schools* (The Plowden Report). London: HMSO.

DfEE/QCA (1999) *The National Curriculum Handbook for Primary Teachers in England*. London: Department for Education and Employment/ Qualifications and Curriculum Authority.

Department for Education and Science (DfES) (1989) *The National Curriculum Handbook for Primary Teachers in England*. London: HMSO.

Galton, M., Simon, B. and Croll, P. (1980) *Inside the Primary Classroom*. London: Routledge and Kegan Paul.

Galton, M., Hargreaves, L., Comber, C., Wall, D. and Pell, T. (1999) *Inside the Primary Classroom: 20 Years On*. London: Routledge.

Laurie, J. (2011) Curriculum planning and preparation for cross-curricular teaching, in T. Kerry (ed.) *Cross-Curricular Teaching in the Primary School*. London: Routledge: 125–41.

Smith, R., Stead, D. and Wilkinson, J. (1984) *CLUES: Science in an Integrated Topic*. Sheffield: PAVIC.

1 Why use a cross-curricular approach to teaching and learning?

Lois Kelly

In this chapter we will look at the broader debate surrounding cross-curricular approaches to teaching and learning. We will look at some links to learning theories that have influenced this approach as well as considering some of the practicalities of using a cross-curricular approach when teaching science in primary schools.

A brief history

The merits of cross-curricular or thematic work in the primary curriculum have been the subject of debate for some considerable time, and have tended to be characterized in the press as a debate about the merits of 'progressive' or 'child-centred' forms of teaching as compared to 'traditional' teaching, in which subjects are taught discretely. Put simply, the emphasis in 'progressive' or 'child-centred' approaches is on helping children to make sense of the world in which they live, whereas 'traditional' approaches tend to place an emphasis on essential knowledge that children need to learn.

Historically, cross-curricular work has been associated with more child-centred, constructivist approaches to primary education, which in the last century was endorsed by the Hadow Report of 1931, the Plowden Report of 1967 and a number of School Council publications in the 1970s. Arguments in support of this approach are based in an understanding of child development. Very young children, at preschool and the lower end of primary school, do not assign particular activities to a particular subject, and therefore this approach more closely mirrors the way they learn. The assertion in the Plowden Report (CACE, 1967: para 555) that 'children's learning does not fit into neat subject categories' is frequently used to support cross-curricular themes or topics although the report did recognize that some discrete subject teaching will be relevant for older primary children. More recently, this view of children's learning moving from broad areas of learning to more discrete subject teaching formed the basis of the primary curriculum proposed by the Independent Review of the Primary Curriculum, commissioned by the last Labour Government (Rose, 2009). According to Carr (2007), this approach is also based on the work of John Dewey, who argued that much knowledge is interrelated. For example, knowledge of the properties of materials combined with knowledge about the climate of different regions of the world helps children to understand differences in the styles of buildings in different regions of the world.

Task 1.1

Choose a common building material such as a brick, concrete or timber.

What are the properties of that material that make it suitable for building with? Think about the strength of the material, whether it is waterproof, how well it will weather, the price and availability.

Find photographs of houses from different regions of the world made from that material. Note the differences in the styles of the buildings. How has the climate influenced the style of building and the choice of materials used?

Look at different houses in your local area and develop a timeline for when they were built. Choose one part of a house, such as the roof or windows. Is the same building material used throughout the timeline?

The 1960s, 1970s and early 1980s saw a move towards organizing the curriculum in primary schools around cross-curricular topics or projects (Carr, 2007), though not to the exclusion of discrete subject teaching, particularly of mathematics and English (Alexander et al., 1992). However, the introduction of the National Curriculum (DfEE/QCA, 1999), with its focus on programmes of study for individual subjects, resulted in a move towards discrete subject teaching in primary schools. This greater emphasis on teaching discrete subjects was further encouraged by successive governments following the 'Three Wise Men' report by Alexander, Rose and Woodhead (1992) which criticized poorly planned topic or thematic work in primary schools that resulted in superficial learning. The fact that this report acknowledged that, when well planned, topic work produced work of a high standard tended to be overlooked.

Although discrete subject teaching became more broadly accepted in primary schools, a ten-year study by Boyle and Bragg (2008) between 1997 and 2007 showed that subjects continued to be taught in a cross-curricular way at least for some of the time, throughout this period. They found that the trend for discrete subject teaching reached a peak following the introduction of the Numeracy and Literacy Strategies and QCA schemes of work, when most subjects were taught as discrete subjects for more than 50 per cent of the time for which they were taught. The study found that from 2002 schools began to reintroduce cross-curricular teaching, often for the pragmatic reason that it enabled them to meet the expectation in the National Curriculum that all children are entitled to a 'coherent, broad and balanced curriculum' (DfEE/QCA, 1999: 4). This trend also coincided with a recognition by Ofsted (2002) that thematic or cross-curricular teaching was a feature of successful primary schools, and at the same time guidance on adopting a more flexible approach to the curriculum, *Designing and Timetabling the Primary Curriculum*, was published (QCA, 2002). More recently, the notion that discrete subject teaching and cross-curricular teaching are mutually exclusive has been challenged by both Alexander (2010: 245–7) and Rose (2009), who advocate a combination of discrete subject teaching and of well planned cross-curricular themes.

> Our primary schools also show that high standards are best secured when essential knowledge and skills are learned both through direct, high-quality subject teaching and also through this content being applied and used in cross-curricular studies.
>
> (Rose, 2009: 2)

Alexander (2010) argues that when planning a curriculum it is important to develop a common understanding of how knowledge is developed. He contends that learning how knowledge is evaluated and tested can be just as relevant to subject disciplines as to interdisciplinary topics. This move towards including cross-curricular approaches in the curriculum can also be seen in the curricula of a number of different countries, for example the Curriculum for Excellence in Scotland (2008), Northern Ireland (2005), and New Zealand (2007). In this chapter we will consider reasons for adopting a cross-curricular approach to teaching and learning and some of the challenges this approach presents.

First, though, we need to consider different interpretations of the term 'cross-curricular teaching and learning', because over the years a variety of different terms have been used in connection with this approach. For example, cross-curricular work has been called 'project work' or 'project-based learning', 'topic' or 'thematic work', 'integrated learning' and 'interdisciplinary learning' (Carr, 2007; Czerniak, 2007). In this book we are primarily concerned with considering how another subject can support and enhance children's learning in science. This may be because the knowledge and understanding learned in that subject complements a particular science topic, or because there are skills common to both subjects. It is not our intention to suggest that cross-curricular study should be limited to making links between two subjects, but we note that a number of recent reports about cross-curricular work emphasize the importance of limiting the number of subjects which contribute to a given theme or topic to ensure that there is a clear focus for children's learning (Ofsted, 2002; Jarvis, 2009; Barnes, 2011: 181–98). Instead, our intention is to consider how individual subjects both enhance and are enhanced by making effective cross-curricular links with science.

Why use a cross-curricular approach in science?

When deciding on which teaching strategy is most appropriate to use in a particular context it is important to consider the view of learning that informs your choice. Both science education and cross-curricular approaches to teaching and learning are informed by a constructivist view of learning. This is based on the proposition that learning is an active mental process in which connections are made between experience, prior knowledge and new ideas, to develop and refine children's knowledge and understanding of a subject or topic. It also emphasizes that the learner is in control of their learning (Pritchard, 2005: 41). In science this view of learning is supported by more than 30 years of research, for example the Children's Learning in Science Project (1984–86) and the SPACE Project (1990–95) (Wellcome Trust, 2005), which show that learning in science is most effective when children are able to see the relevance of the science they are learning and when it is meaningful to them. Making science interesting and relevant to children is one of the key features of effective science teaching and learning (Harlen, 2006: 9; Wellcome Trust, 2008), and developing effective cross-curricular links helps children to appreciate the relevance of scientific ideas and skills (Jarvis, 2009). Schools may also have a more pragmatic reason for developing cross-curricular links, as Boyle and Bragg (2008) discovered. They found that developing cross-curricular links enabled the schools to develop a broad and balanced curriculum, although Alexander (2010: 260) cautions against using manageability of the curriculum as a reason for making links between different areas of the curriculum.

Concerns about cross-curricular work

When discussing a cross-curricular approach to teaching and learning it is important to keep in mind the concerns that have been raised by critics of this approach. These are that:

- it lacks rigour and pupils may not develop essential subject-specific skills (Muijs and Reynolds, 2011)
- subjects lose their identity (Czerniak, 2007; Parkinson, 2010; Barnes, 2011).
- learning is superficial and fragmentary (Alexander et al., 1992)
- tenuous links are made between subjects (Jarvis, 2009; Laurie, 2011: 128).

What has given rise to these concerns? Given that one of the advantages of cross-curricular work is that children are able to apply skills developed in one subject to other subjects, why is there concern that children may not develop subject-specific skills? Is this due to poor planning or might this be caused by limited opportunities to develop knowledge and understanding of these subject-specific skills? Is the concern about superficial and fragmentary learning in topics due to teachers being overambitious when planning topics, and making links between too many subject areas given the timescale available for the work? Is it, as Thomas (2012) suggests, because teachers have not been encouraged to be curriculum developers? Recently concern has been raised over the quality of teaching of foundation subjects in the primary curriculum (Alexander, 2010: 244–5) due to the emphasis on literacy and numeracy, both in primary schools and in professional development courses for primary teachers. The concern about superficial and fragmentary teaching may then not be specific to cross-curricular or topic work, but relate to the status of a subject within the curriculum. Do subjects lose their identity in cross-curricular projects because when planning a topic the focus has been on the product rather than the process of learning and the unique contribution of each subject to that learning?

Advantages of cross-curricular work

Ofsted (2002) noted that one of the features of successful primary schools is the ability of teachers to plan opportunities for children to apply the knowledge and skills learned in one subject to other subjects. This leads me to ask, 'What is it that makes cross-curricular work a successful approach for teaching and learning?' As has already been suggested, cross-curricular teaching and learning has strong links with the constructivist view of learning, as children work collaboratively and learn from their own direct experience (Hayes, 2010). Adopting a cross-curricular approach to teaching and learning requires careful consideration of what we mean when we talk about 'knowledge'. Is it possible to develop a good understanding of any given event or idea by simply being able to quote relevant facts or information? Alexander (2010: 248) points out that learning facts or information is not the same as developing knowledge. Kerry (2011), who is a strong advocate for cross-curricular work, argues that individual subject disciplines only give a partial insight into a particular topic or problem, and that to enable them to fully understand the problem, children need to be encouraged to draw together insights from different subjects. This notion that knowledge is interrelated is supported by Carr (2007), who traced it back to Dewey's views that knowledge is useful to help develop an understanding of our experiences rather than simply learning reported facts or information.

Well planned cross-curricular work helps children make sense of their learning because knowledge and skills learned in one subject are used to reinforce and support learning in other subjects (Hayes, 2010). Consider, for example, teaching children about measurement in mathematics. In which other subjects will children use this knowledge and develop their ability to make accurate measurements? How does making accurate measurements when cooking or when making an artefact in design and technology help develop children's competence with the concept of measurement in mathematics? Barnes (2011) and Savage (2011), though, point out that to be effective the links between subjects need to be made explicit, because it should not be assumed that skills and knowledge learned in one context will be transferred to a different context (Pritchard, 2005: 88). This is not a simple matter because it requires teachers to have good knowledge of a range of different subjects, which includes being sensitive to the culture or values of a subject as well as the concepts, knowledge and skills inherent in that subject (Savage, 2011: 40). A recurring theme in the case studies and reports about cross-curricular work (Ofsted, 2008; Barnes, 2011; Laurie, 2011) is the need to ensure that links between subjects are authentic, because if a subject does not fit logically into the theme or topic the skills and concepts of that subject may not be adequately addressed (Jarvis, 2009; Muijs and Reynolds, 2011), compromising learning in the subject.

Although Venville et al. (2002), while acknowledging the concerns of subject specialists that children's understanding of subject-specific knowledge was less secure when they were working on a cross-curricular project, suggest that this may be balanced by an improvement in other aspects of learning, such as developing research and problem-solving skills. Kerry (2011: 20–35) also argues that cross-curricular work helps children develop thinking skills such as problem-solving and reasoning, a view supported by Barnes (2011), because children not only apply knowledge and skills learned in one subject to another, but will also synthesize information and ideas from a range of sources. Learning to make links is one of the attributes of a good learner (Claxton, 2002: 27). Also relevant to this discussion is the notion that in real life insights from different subject disciplines are used to solve problems (Muijs and Reynolds, 2011: 282) and so giving children opportunities to work on cross-curricular topics develops skills that will be useful in their future careers.

One of the features of a constructivist view of learning, based on the work of both Bruner and Vygotsky, is that learning is a collaborative process both between children and between children and their teacher. Consequently language has a central role in developing thinking and learning (Mercer, 2000; Alexander, 2008). As with all teaching, when planning cross-curricular work we need to be aware of how language will support children's learning. This is discussed in more detail in Chapter 2. All subjects have their own particular language culture, and Savage (2011: 99) highlights the importance of ensuring consistency in the use of language in cross-curricular study while at the same time ensuring that the technical language of the discrete subjects is used accurately. However, for children, one of the benefits of cross-curricular work is that the language demands are related (Jarvis, 2009), which is an advantage in communities where English is not their mother tongue.

A common theme in much of the recent literature about cross-curricular work is that it improves pupils' motivation and engagement, as learning is placed in a context that is both interesting and relevant to the learner (QCA, 2005; Barnes, 2011; Muijs and Reynolds, 2011: 282; Savage, 2011). Some, though, would question whether it is possible for all children to be interested and motivated by any one theme or topic. Perhaps one reason that cross-curricular work improves motivation and engagement is the breadth of study. For some children it will be the science that interests them, whereas for others it will be another subject such as geography, history or art. Fifty years on, I can still remember learning about chocolate at primary school. I was fascinated to learn about the Aztec rituals related to drinking chocolate and how the Conquistadors introduced chocolate to Europe, as well as learning about the changes to chocolate as it was processed. Rennie et al. (2011) found that when children worked on a cross-curricular project, the motivation for learning was mastering a task or solving a problem rather than gaining a good grade in a test or exam. Another reason that cross-curricular work is motivating is that it allows for more independent, learner-led exploration of the topic (Muijs and Reynolds, 2011). This appeal to the emotional aspects of learning resonates with a growing understanding of how emotions affect learning. Many readers will recognize that they are much more prepared to make the effort to learn something that is thought to be 'difficult' when they are interested in the topic, and it is more difficult to learn when they are not interested or do not see the point of learning something. Many will also recognize the 'buzz' they get when the children in their class are engaged and show interest and enthusiasm for a particular lesson or topic, whether this is in a discrete subject or as part of a cross-curricular topic. Curran (2008: 61–6), writing about how the brain 'works', states that 'learning is directed and controlled by the emotional / limbic brain' and 'the emotional self is centrally involved in the vast majority of things you learn'. It should be noted, however, that all teaching, whether of discrete subjects or of cross-curricular topics, should endeavour to make learning 'feel good'. The benefits for children's personal and social development of working on cross-curricular projects were also noted by Ofsted (2008) in a survey of schools which had adopted a cross-curricular or thematic approach to the curriculum.

Challenges when developing cross-curricular work

Having considered some of the benefits of using a cross-curricular approach to enhance children's learning, we also recognize that there are challenges. Several reports make the point that developing cross-curricular work requires carefully designed professional development for teachers, and time needs to be allocated for this (Ofsted, 2008; Jarvis, 2009; Thomas, 2012). This need for professional development, as the report from the Royal Society for the Arts (RSA) points out (Thomas, 2012), arises because many teachers have received little or no training in designing the curriculum for their school because of the emphasis, since the introduction of the National Curriculum, on discrete subject teaching and, particularly in primary schools, the reliance on detailed schemes of work. As a consequence, many of the newer entrants to the teaching profession have had limited experience of cross-curricular work, either as pupils or subsequently during their school-based training (Barnes and Shirley, 2007; Aston and Jackson, 2010), and as a result tend to compartmentalize learning. The need for primary teachers to develop an understanding of the holistic nature of the primary curriculum during initial teacher education is highlighted by Alexander (2010: 424). Although the professional development that is needed to support curriculum developments may come from outside agencies (Thomas, 2012), schools that have successfully introduced thematic or cross-curricular work have done so using the expertise of the teachers in their school (Ofsted, 2008).

One of the challenges when planning cross-curricular work is maintaining an appropriate balance between the subjects which contribute to the study, so having a clear rationale for including subjects in the theme or topic helps to maintain the rigour of the study. Jarvis (2009) notes that there is a risk that one subject may have a higher profile because the enthusiasm of the pupils drives the learning in one particular direction. However, Laurie (2011) notes that for some topics it may be appropriate to have a lead subject which drives the particular study, while Barnes (2011) recommends keeping to a maximum of three or four subjects which contribute to a cross-curricular theme or study to maintain the integrity of the study. At the risk of stating the obvious, developing clear learning objectives also helps establish cross-curricular links that focus on the learning not simply the activity or product (Savage, 2011: 61). Studies have also shown that using the National Curriculum programmes of study to inform the planning of cross-curricular work is a successful strategy to help ensure an appropriate balance (Ofsted, 2008; Jarvis, 2009). An advantage of this is that it may help to address the concerns about a lack of progression in children's learning which were raised about 'topic work' in the 'Three Wise Men' report (Alexander et al., 1992: paras 67–8). We will discuss planning in greater detail in Chapter 10.

A second challenge when developing cross-curricular work relates to time. Time needs to be allocated in three different aspects of cross-curricular work. In the first instance, when planning a cross-curricular theme or topic teachers need time to research it and to explore the links between the different subjects. Savage (2011) talks about teachers needing a deep understanding of the culture of each subject, by which he means not only what is learned but also how it is taught/learned, and how it affects the lives of both the teacher and the pupil. For example, we have already hinted at the need to consider the language demands of different subjects. Planning also takes longer, especially when the topic is new, because the resources – both physical resources and human resources – may not be established in the school. It is an opportunity to explore and develop relationships with organizations or individuals who can support children's learning. For example there are many in the 'older generation' who can give first-hand accounts of their life in the Second World War. The second consideration about time is classroom-based, and focuses on managing the timetable flexibly to enable children to become engaged, and hopefully engrossed, in the topic. There may be a need at one point for an intense focus, such as a whole day, on the topic, while at a different stage it may be more appropriate to focus for an hour or two on one particular aspect. Finally it is important to allow time for an evaluation of the topic from both the children's perspective and the teacher's perspective.

Assessment is a further challenge for teachers developing a cross-curricular approach. Both Ofsted (2008) and Kerry (2011: 12) assert that well planned cross-curricular work can have a positive impact on achievements, which is evidenced through tests and external exams. However studies by both Venville et al. (2002) and Rennie et al. (2011) discuss the difficulty of assessing children's learning when using a cross-curricular approach. They point out that traditional forms of assessment are limited because they tend to focus on assessing subject-specific knowledge and concepts and do not take account of how children apply subject-specific knowledge. However, this should not be an excuse for not assessing children's learning. As much of the literature on assessment for learning notes, an important feature of any assessment is being able to clearly identify the learning intentions at any stage of a topic. Although it is an obvious statement to make, turning this into the reality that informs effective teaching and learning requires a good understanding of the skills and knowledge that will be developed and applied in any given topic. This is discussed in more detail in Chapter 11.

Conclusion

This chapter has given a very brief history of cross-curricular approaches to teaching and learning in primary education, and considered how constructivist learning theories support this approach and consequently are closely allied to the research into effective science education. It has recognized that there are challenges for teachers when adopting a cross-curricular approach and that there is no clear message as to how to achieve effective cross-curricular learning. Decisions about when and how to make links between subjects will depend on the educational purpose for adopting this approach.

References

Alexander, R. (2008) *Towards Dialogic Teaching: Rethinking Classroom Talk.* Fourth edition. Thirsk: Dialogos.

Alexander, R. (ed.) (2010) *Children, their World, their Education: Final Report and Recommendations of the Cambridge Primary Review.* London: Routledge.

Alexander, R.J., Rose, A.J. and Woodhead, C. (1992) *Curriculum Organisation and Classroom Practice in Primary Schools: A Discussion Paper.* London: Department of Education and Science.

Aston, S. and Jackson, D. (2010) Blurring the boundaries or muddying the waters? *Design and Technology Education: An International Journal,* 14(1): 68–76.

Barnes, J. (2011) *Cross-Curricular Learning 3–14.* Second edition. London: Sage.

Barnes, J. and Shirley, I. (2007) Strangely familiar: cross-curricular teaching and creative thinking in teacher education. *Improving Schools*, 10(2): 162–79.

Boyle, B. and Bragg, J. (2008) Making primary connections: the cross-curriculum story. *Curriculum Journal*, 19(1): 5–21.

Central Advisory Council for Education (CACE) (1967) *Children and their Primary Schools* (The Plowden Report). London: HMSO.

Carr, D. (2007) Towards an educationally meaningful curriculum: epistemic holism and knowledge integration revisited. *British Journal of Educational Studies*, 55(1): 3–20.

Claxton, G. (2002) *Building Learning Power*. Bristol: TLO.

Curran, A. (2008) *The Little Book of Big Stuff about the Brain*. Carmarthen: Crown House.

Curriculum for Excellence (2008) Available at http://www.education-scotland.gov.uk/thecurriculum/whatiscurriculumforexcellence/index.asp [accessed 29 May 2012].

Czerniak, C.M. (2007) Interdisciplinary science teaching, in S.K. Abell and N.G. Lederman (eds.), *Handbook of Research on Science Education*. Mahwah, NJ: Lawrence Erlbaum Associates: 537–59.

DfEE/QCA (1999) *The National Curriculum Handbook for Primary Teachers in England*. London: Department for Education and Employment/ Qualifications and Curriculum Authority.

Harlen, W. (2006) *Teaching Learning and Assessing Science 5–12*. Fourth edition. London: Sage.

Hayes, D. (2010) The seductive charms of a cross-curricular approach. *Education 3–13: International Journal of Primary, Elementary and Early Years Education*, 38(4): 381–7.

Jarvis, T. (2009) Promoting creative science cross-curricular work through an in-service programme. *School Science Review*, 90(332): 39–46.

Kerry, T. (ed.) (2011) *Cross-Curricular Teaching in the Primary School: Planning and Facilitating Imaginative Lessons*. London: Routledge.

Laurie, J. (2011) Curriculum planning and preparation for cross-curricular teaching, in T. Kerry (ed.) *Cross-curricular Teaching in the Primary School*. London: Routledge: 125–41.

Mercer, N. (2000) *Words and Minds: How we Use Language to Think*. London: Routledge.

Muijs, D. and Reynolds, D. (2011) *Effective Teaching: Evidence and Practice*. London: Sage.

The New Zealand Curriculum (2007) Available at http://nzcurriculum.tki.org.nz/Curriculum-documents/The-New-Zealand-Curriculum [accessed 29 May 2012].

Northern Ireland Curriculum (2005) *The Revised Northern Ireland Primary Curriculum: Key Stages 1 and 2 (2005)*. Belfast: NI Curriculum. Available at http://www.nicurriculum.org.uk/docs/background/curriculum_review/FINAL_WebVersion_PrimaryPropsals_KS12.pdf [accessed 29 May 2012].

Ofsted (2002) *The Curriculum in Successful Primary Schools*. London: Ofsted.

Ofsted (2008) *Curriculum Innovation in Schools*. London: Ofsted. Available at http://www.ofsted.gov.uk/resources/curriculum-innovation-schools [accessed 29 May 2012].

Parkinson, E. (2010) Where next in a world of cross-curricular primary education? *Design and Technology Education: An International Journal*, 15(1): 14–23.

Pritchard, A. (2005) *Ways of Learning: Learning Theories and Learning Styles in the Classroom*. Abingdon: David Fulton.

QCA (2002) *Designing and Timetabling the Primary Curriculum: A Practical Guide for Key Stages 1 and 2*. London: QCA. Available at https://www.education.gov.uk/publications/standard/publicationDetail/Page1/QCA/02/912 [accessed 20 Feb 2012].

QCA (2005) *Customise your Curriculum*. Available at http://webarchive.nationalarchives.gov.uk/20100612050234/http://qca.org.uk/qca_5198.aspx [accessed 15 Feb 2012].

Rennie, L.J., Venville, G. and Wallace, J. (2011) Learning science in an integrated classroom: finding balance through theoretical triangulation. *Journal of Curriculum Studies*, 43(2): 139–62.

Rose, J. (2009) *Independent Review of the Primary Curriculum: Final Report*. London: DCSF. Available at https://www.education.gov.uk/publications/standard/publicationDetail/Page1/DCSF-00499-2009 [accessed 14 Feb 2012].

Savage, J. (2011) *Cross-curricular Teaching and Learning in the Secondary School*. London: Routledge.

Thomas, L. (2012) *Re-thinking the Importance of Teaching: Curriculum and Collaboration in an Era of Localism*. London: RSA. Available at http://www.thersa.org/__data/assets/pdf_file/0008/570716/RSA-Re-thinking-the-importance-of-teaching.pdf [accessed 17 July 2012].

Venville, G.J., Wallace, J., Rennie, L.J. and Malone, J.A. (2002) Curriculum integration: eroding the high ground of science as a subject. *Studies in Science Education*, 37(1): 43–83.

Wellcome Trust (2005) *Primary Horizons: Starting Out in Science*. London: Wellcome Trust. Available at http://www.wellcome.ac.uk/primary-horizons [accessed 8 Mar 12].

Wellcome Trust (2008) *Perspectives on Education: Primary Science*. London: Wellcome Trust. Available at http://www.wellcome.ac.uk/perspectives [accessed 8 Mar 12].

2   English enhancing science

Alison Brade

Literacy across the curriculum is not a new idea. It is widely acknowledged that in order to access other areas of the curriculum pupils need to have a good command of literacy skills. However, it is not just about practising their literacy skills in other subjects but about explicitly teaching particular aspects of literacy within other subjects. Wray (2006: xi) identifies three clear aims for teaching literacy across the curriculum:

1   It should broaden and enhance children's command of literacy skills by giving them a range of different contexts in which to use and practise these skills.
2   It should locate the teaching of literacy skills central to a particular subject within that subject.
3   It should enhance the learning of the subject and children's motivations towards that learning.

Science, as an enquiry-based subject, provides a meaningful context in which to develop children's group interaction skills. Group interaction requires the participants to develop a range of different types of talk (Corden, 2000). Through discussion, children will be investigating, selecting, sorting, planning, predicting, exploring, explaining, reporting and evaluating. As such, Alexander suggests that 'talk is arguably the true foundation of learning' (Alexander, 2008: 5). Many of these types of talk involve asking questions – this is, in fact, a key skill of exploratory and investigative talk. Therefore, questioning needs to be taught and opportunities for children to ask questions need to be identified.

In science, pupils need to ask questions of the world in which they live in order to make sense of it. Teachers' use of questions has been well documented (Galton et al., 1999) and it has been noted that in the majority of cases it is the use of low-level questions that dominates much interaction in the classroom – approximately 80 to 90 per cent. Children's use of questions has not been documented in the same way. Both the Cambridge Review of the National Curriculum (Alexander, 2010) and the National Curriculum Review Expert Panel Report (DfE, 2011) state that oracy has not been given the place in the primary curriculum which is required to effectively develop children's cognitive skills. They identify that:

> There is a compelling body of evidence that highlights a connection between oral development, cognitive development and educational attainment. Over the past four decades successive reviews, enquiries and development projects have also explored the crucial nature of oral capability within education.
>
> (DfE, 2011: 52)

Children need to be taught how to frame questions in order to investigate both their world and the texts they read. Bloom's revised categories of cognitive processes range from low-level recall to higher-level synthesis (creating) (Anderson and Krathwohl, 2001). Bloom originally intended his taxonomy to be a support for teachers when identifying learning objectives for lessons. He believed that it would facilitate a much deeper level of engagement and interaction, and therefore learning, among pupils and their teachers. Traditionally, teachers have provided the question words: *who?, what?, where?, when?, why?, how?* as stems for children to generate their own questions. Both Riley (2000) and Wray (2006) suggest providing children with these question words to scaffold the writing of questions. However, these very often result in lower order questions being composed. If we want children to engage with learning at a deeper level we need to support them in generating higher order questions.

Scaffolding using question stems is an effective way of encouraging and supporting children's questioning. As mentioned earlier, the most commonly provided question stems are: *who?, what?, when?, where?* and *why?*, resulting in basic recall. However, if we use Bloom's taxonomy and provide question stems which require cognitive functioning at higher levels, this will support children's development both in oral language skills and in science. By introducing auxiliary verbs, such as *is, did, can, would, will, might*, to follow the question words we can ask questions at a higher cognitive level. For example, *what might?* immediately requires a much higher level of cognitive thought than *what is?* Thomson (2011) researched using Bloom's taxonomy to support children's generation of questions in science. He was eager to develop ways so that it was the children rather than the teacher that asked the questions. He devised prompt cards based on the different levels of Bloom's taxonomy. These provided structured question stems for the children to ask questions which other children could then investigate and answer. He explains that the choice of question stems depended not only on ability but also on the activity, as not all levels were appropriate for each activity. The recorded impact was a greater number of children achieving level 4+ and 5+ in the science SATs at the end of Key Stage 2. This demonstrates that explicitly teaching children how to ask questions is beneficial to both their English learning and their science learning.

Scientific study does not and should not rely solely on the use of secondary sources. It should also involve scientific enquiry of a practical nature, and again children's questioning skills are an important aspect of investigations. One of the ways children's questioning skills can be developed for scientific enquiry is through dialogic teaching. Dialogic teaching is collective, reciprocal, cumulative and supportive (Alexander, 2010). It is through collaborative discussions about activities (including teachers and pupils) that teachers can model the use of exploratory talk and investigative questions. In this way, learning can be reciprocal. These discussions are not unplanned but are *'purposeful*: teachers plan and steer classroom talk with specific educational goals in view' (Alexander, 2010: 306) – in this case, developing children's use of exploratory talk and questioning. In 1999 Agar, Jones and Simpson carried out an investigation into how teachers could support children in generating questions. Teachers used focused discussion to model the types of question the children might ask during scientific enquiry. While working alongside the children they asked questions such as 'Why is that thing floating and that thing sinking?', 'How can we make that stronger?', thereby following the principles of dialogic teaching. When they analysed their results they discovered that the children who were involved in the study stayed on task longer, demonstrated a greater understanding and devised higher quality investigations (Agar et al., 1999). Therefore, by developing the children's questioning skills, the children not only become more proficient in the use of more complex language structures but they also begin to 'think like a scientist'. In the science classroom, activities can be organized in ways that promote speaking and listening, and thereby thinking, because 'Learning to talk like scientists provides children with a transferable learning tool with which to question, assert, explain, hypothesize, reflect ... and more' (Loxley et al., 2010: 37).

In order for dialogic teaching to be effective, the role of the teacher needs to be managed carefully. It is important that the teacher is seen as a member of the group rather than the leader. Harlen and Qualter (2009: 102) describe the teacher's role as one which provides 'positive encouragement of reflective teaching'. They state that teachers should avoid dominating the discussion and join in *as part of* the group; listen to children's contributions and use a variety of techniques which encourage children to elaborate on their contributions, such as 'I see' and 'Yes?'; ask children to explain their thinking and probe their contribution to help them clarify what they mean. When asking the children questions, they also suggest that using person-centred questions will aid discussion more than subject-centred questions (Harlen and Qualter, 2009: 145). This is because subject-centred questions require a level of knowledge and indicate a 'right' answer, in that they ask *'Why do ...?'* whereas person-centred questions explore the child's thinking and encourage exploratory talk: *'Why do you think ...?'*

When carrying out practical investigations children are often asked to work in groups, which requires them to engage in collaborative talk. This type of talk – group interaction – is often described as being more symmetrical than teacher–pupil interaction. It has also been observed as being 'often uncooperative, off-task, inequitable and ultimately unproductive' (Mercer et al., 2004). It is suggested that this is because the children are not given specific guidance in how to engage in group discussion. Mercer has been involved in a number of projects which have looked into developing interaction in the classroom with a view to improving attainment. The 'Thinking Together' projects all ensure that children are taught explicitly about exploratory talk, they devise ground rules for talk alongside their teachers, the teacher acts as a model and guide for the children, and the children work in groups of three (Dawes, 2000).

In an earlier study Dawes and colleagues examined group interaction and exploratory talk, and as a result identified the following ground rules:

- The group takes responsibility for decisions
- All relevant information is shared
- The group seeks to reach agreement
- Reasons are expected
- Challenges are accepted
- Alternatives are discussed before a decision is taken
- All in the group are encouraged to speak by other group members
(Grugeon et al., 1999: 90)

Rather than imposing these ground rules on the children, it was decided that they should be negotiated with the children. As a result a child-friendly version of the rules was developed:

1 Everyone should have a chance to talk.
2 Everyone's ideas should be carefully considered.
3 Each member of the group should be asked
   a) What do you think?
   b) Why do you think that?
4 We will look at and listen to the person talking.
5 After discussion, the group will agree on their idea before they enter it in to the computer.

The research team discovered that the children's interactions were more task-related and that exploratory talk was more evident. They also noticed that individual children's reasoning skills had been enhanced.

Support materials from the Primary National Strategy have also suggested that children from Year 4 onwards could be given specific roles in the group, such as chair, scribe, reporter and facilitator. However, simply giving out roles or rules is often not enough. Working with children it quickly became apparent that they also needed support with what the roles meant and the type of things people who undertook these roles might say. For example, a jigsawing method was used, where all the chairs grouped together to identify what they thought their role might entail, and then note down the sorts of things they might say in order to carry out this role. The children identified that the chair should make sure everyone stayed on task – or as they said 'stuck to doing the job' – that the job was completed in the time given and that everyone was clear what the job was. As a result they then identified some ideas for talk, for example 'We seem to be wandering off the job – let's get back to what we are supposed to be doing', 'Should we move on to the next thing?' and 'We've only got five minutes left'. The other roles worked in the same way. Each group then made a poster which was clearly displayed in the classroom. Having carried out this 'talk lesson', the children were then provided with a group task to complete. Observations demonstrated that the children enjoyed taking on these roles and were beginning to understand them. They were also seen to refer to the posters they made for ideas of things they might say. It was noted that the children remained on task and were focused.

Questioning was also identified by the National Reading Panel (2000) as one of five skills which need to be taught in order to develop children's comprehension. The five skills are predicting, *questioning*, clarifying, imagining and summarizing.

Taking questioning as one of the key comprehension skills, it becomes clear that this is a skill that is common to both English and science. In English, children need to ask questions of the texts they read, and of other people they talk to in order to clarify meaning. Comprehension is a highly interactive process between the text and the reader. Sweet and Snow (2003) describe it as having three elements:

- the reader, who is doing the comprehending
- the text that is to be comprehended
- the activity in which comprehension is a part.

These three elements all interact within a socio-cultural context. When considering this context there are two text-related elements that need to be considered in particular with regard to non-fiction texts: the non-fiction schema and the topic. 'Such schemas are a kind of road map that can be used to guide comprehension processes' (Primary National Strategy, 2006). Also, if the reader has some familiarity with the topic being read about this can aid comprehension.

Therefore, reading comprehension can be improved by activating the pupils' prior knowledge. The Primary National Strategy documented a number of ways in which this could be achieved: brainstorming, KWL grids (what I **k**now, what I **w**ant to know and what I have **l**earned), mind mapping, and drawing pictures. Wray (2006) uses a KWL grid to help children move from their prior knowledge to generating questions to be researched. He suggests taking statements that the children have written in the 'K' column and turning them into questions using the 'W' question words. For example, 'Plants have leaves' would become '*Why* do plants have leaves?' In this way, using Bloom's taxonomy the children would be taking their learning from level 1 'recall' to level 2 'understanding'. Of course, once the questions have been identified the children then need to research them. For some science topics this might mean using secondary sources (texts). Both Wray and Lewis (1997) and Neate (1992, 2000) state that more often than not children then resort to copying because they have not been taught the skills of note-taking.

Neate discusses a variety of note-taking strategies which can be used effectively with primary school children. These include drawing pictures, using grids, underlining and making patterns. Each method of note-taking is suitable for different non-fiction genres. She makes the very important point that before any of the note-taking strategies are used the children should be clear about the 'questions' they are researching.

Non-fiction texts often use vocabulary that is familiar to children, but in a non-fiction context it can take on an entirely different meaning. For example, when discussing 'the milky way' during a topic on 'Earth and Space', the children may well have an image of a chocolate bar in their minds. This is another reason why it is important for teachers to activate children's prior knowledge of a topic before embarking on reading non-fiction texts. The importance of introducing children to scientific vocabulary has been documented in all versions of the National Curriculum. For the teacher this raises the question of when to introduce particular vocabulary and the level of understanding of the vocabulary. Harlen and Qualter (2009: 107) suggest that 'most scientific words (such as evaporation, dissolving, power, reflection) label concepts which can be understood at varying levels of complexity'. Therefore they suggest that 'we should, perhaps, accept children's "loose" use of words as a starting point to development of a more refined and scientific understanding of the word'. They go on to suggest criteria for teachers to use to decide when to introduce new terminology. Teachers will need to consider whether:

- the child has had experience of the event or phenomenon which it covers
- the word is needed at the time
- the word is going to help the child to link related things to each other (since words often give clues to these links).

(Harlen and Qualter, 2009)

Of course, speaking and listening will not be the only 'English' activities children will be engaged in when learning science. They will also be reading and writing non-fiction texts. It is important that children are provided with a context when teaching non-fiction reading and writing. One reason for this is that, as Palmer and Corbett (2003) suggest, non-fiction writing has two horses before the cart! – one of the horses being the language knowledge and skills, the other being knowledge of the content to be written about. An efficient way of managing this in a very overcrowded curriculum is to 'borrow' topics from other curriculum areas. So, for instance, when the children are studying 'the Earth and beyond' in science, they can use texts relating to this to explore how non-fiction texts work and how they are organized, as well as developing the skills of skimming, scanning, note-taking and writing, in addition to developing their comprehension skills associated with non-fiction texts. However, it is more than just 'borrowing' topics from other subjects. Moore and Moore (1989) found that when you integrate science learning with strategies for reading non-fiction texts more effectively, children's learning in *both* science *and* literacy are enhanced.

Since the introduction of the National Literacy Strategy in 1998, teachers have become more familiar with the range of non-fiction genres. Each one has its own specific structure and language features which children need to be taught. When looking at science it is possible to see how children might encounter each of the six non-fiction genres: *non-chronological reports* when reading and writing about specific phenomena such as the solar system, *recounts* when retelling or writing up an experiment that has been carried out, *explanations* when reading and writing about a process such as the water cycle, *instructions* when reading about how to carry out a particular activity such as making an electrical circuit, *discussions* when considering the advantages and disadvantages of space exploration or healthy diets, and *persuasive texts* when reading and writing about environmental issues. The work of the Australian genre theorists has identified that although an individual can read one particular type of text and has mastered the art of decoding, it cannot be assumed that they can automatically transfer these skills to other text types. This is because each different genre requires specific reading strategies in order to fully comprehend it.

Using science as a stimulus for children's poetry writing

Poetry and science appear to be two entirely different disciplines. However, they both share a key skill: observation. Observation is the receiving of information from the world through the senses. It is the beginning of the investigation process.

At first the topic of yeast might seem to be the most unlikely subject for poetry writing. However, any topic, if approached in the right way, can help develop children's observational skills and result in the production of some interesting poems.

As part of their initial professional development, a group of PGCE students were introduced to a cross-curricular project involving English, science and art. They were initially shown some magnified images of yeast but they were deliberately not told what the images were. First of all they were asked to write a list of as many adjectives as they could think of to describe the image in front of them. (This relates to level 1 of Bloom's taxonomy.) At first they struggled and the responses were limited to describing the colour: yellow, gold, green, brown. This demonstrated that they were 'looking' but not 'seeing'. To encourage closer observation, the students were then asked to describe the shapes they could see and the textures. They were also directed to look more closely at the colours for more detailed descriptions of shade and tone, light and dark. This resulted in far richer vocabulary: oval, ochre, dimpled, demonstrating that observation is a skill which needs to be nurtured. As Johnston states, 'observation is best developed through structured experiences' (Johnston, 2009). At this stage, with the support of a colleague from the science team, scientific vocabulary was introduced such as 'buds'.

It became clear that if the students needed support in 'observing' the images, then so would children. The approach taken was dialogic teaching. Interaction, both teacher–pupil and pupil–pupil, is pivotal to the learning process and the quality of responses. However, there is a great deal of research which demonstrates that interaction is often underexploited as an effective tool for teaching and learning. Much of the talk, especially between teacher and pupil, is still didactic in nature despite the extensive research which has been undertaken in this field (Galton et al., 1999). During the activity with the students genuine discussions took place, both student–student and tutor–student, about the colours, shapes, tones and textures that could be seen. The interaction was truly reciprocal, in that everyone bounced ideas off each other, and cumulative, in that the ideas built upon contributions made.

The next stage was to compare what the students could see with other phenomena, taking the questions to level 2 of Bloom's taxonomy. Comparing objects requires closer observation and making links with prior knowledge. Rather than asking the students to generate a list of similes, the interaction took a natural progression by asking questions such as 'what can you think of that is round like that/bumpy like that?' The students knew they were generating similes and realized that in this way they could introduce figurative language to children without having to teach the terminology. Metalanguage is useful and makes discussion of texts easier, but using it should not become a barrier to children writing expressively. The aim of learning such devices is to empower children and provide them with a wealth of choices for self-expression.

A traditional textbook approach to teaching similes is often limited to learning those which have become clichés, such as 'as black as coal' and 'as quiet as a mouse'. By asking the students 'What else does it look like?', their imaginations were able to come up with a surprisingly rich source of ideas. Finally, looking at the image as a whole the students were asked 'What does this remind you of?' This helped generate metaphor.

The abstract images of yeast enabled the students' imaginations to generate similes and metaphors without any boundaries. Because they were unfamiliar with the image they were not constrained by preconceived ideas. This in itself encouraged closer observation. The descriptive language the students generated was based on what they could see rather than what they could remember, which can be the case when observing familiar images.

To turn their collections of adjectives, similes and metaphors into poems, the students needed to make choices, select and organize their work: level 4 of Bloom's taxonomy. In order to facilitate this part of the composition process the students needed to be familiar with the structures and features of poetry.

Following the teaching sequence of writing, it is imperative that children are read to, and read a variety of poems before they are asked to compose their own. For this reason the classroom should be 'poetry-rich', providing children with a whole range of poetry anthologies, both single-author and collections, in which to immerse themselves. This will give them models of the different poetic structures and examples of a range of techniques that poets use.

To facilitate children's understanding of the range of techniques available to them, teachers need to discuss the poems they read with children. However, this should be done in a way that encourages children to engage with the poems rather than simply deconstruct them or carry out a parsing activity, which often results in 'killing' the poem and making it complex and therefore something to dislike. As Hull suggests:

> This is not talk like, 'Can you see a metaphor in that line?' or
> 'What was the writer's intention when he wrote: "The fair breeze
> blew/The white foam flew/The furrow followed free ..."?' It is
> not based on the teacher's cross-examination of a child to see
> if they 'know'. It is a conversation, in which the teacher's most
> 'analytical' question might be something like, after a couple of
> readings of a poem, 'Did you like that?' or 'Was there anything
> you liked in that poem?'
>
> (Hull, 2010: 2)

This again takes us back to dialogic teaching. By asking questions such
as these we are moving away from, as Alexander (2008: 106) calls it, the
game of 'guess what the teacher is thinking'. Teachers and children are
exploring the poem together. This can also take away teachers' fear of
teaching poetry.

Before the first composition activity, the students were told that the
images were of yeast cells and had carried out scientific experiments with
yeast. It was a 'shared write' using the students' adjectives. Each adjective had been written on a sticky note, which helped with the selection/
deselection process (Figure 2.1). They were asked to select three adjectives

Figure 2.1 We are choosing adjectives we have written on sticky notes to
use in our poem

Figure 2.2 We are planning our poem. We have connected our sticky notes together to make a poem

which they thought sounded good together. This was then made a little more challenging by introducing the idea of alliteration. At this point, a very interesting observation was made. One group had decided to deselect adjectives which began with 'hard' sounds. When asked why, they explained that yeast was a soft object and like jelly, and therefore they had decided to only use adjectives which began with soft sounds (Figure 2.2).

A further project was undertaken with undergraduate student teachers. This time it took the form of a field trip, and the theme was rocks. Rather than looking at images of rocks, the students were able to observe them in situ. The same process was followed, starting with describing the rocks. This time, though, the students were encouraged to also make use of their senses of hearing and smell. Also, in order to observe more closely, they were provided with magnifying glasses (Figure 2.3). The students had already carried out some classification activities in science and had been introduced to some geological language such as *glacial, granular, crystallized*. They were encouraged to identify these features in the rocks they were observing. When describing the yeast, it had been noted that the students' vocabulary when describing colours was quite limited. Therefore colour charts from well known paint manufacturers were introduced to encourage a more adventurous use of colour vocabulary (Figure 2.4). Scaffolding the activity in this way resulted in closer observation.

In addition, certain poems were selected as models for the students to copy poetic structures. The poems were selected because they made use of particular poetic features. Roger McGough's (1999) *The Reader of this*

Figure 2.3 Making a close observation of rocks in situ with a hand-held microscope

Poem was selected for its use of simile, Wes Magee's (2006) *What is the Sun?* for its use of metaphor, Roger McGough's (2000) *Haiku* was chosen as an example of a haiku, and Anita Marie Sackett's (2000) *Estuary* as an example of an acrostic list poem. The students were given the choice of which of the model poems they wanted to use, and in a short space of time were able to compose poems using the rocks as a stimulus.

There were some key issues that emerged from the project. One was the subject knowledge the students needed in order to support children in composing poetry. This was the case for both the structures and features of poetry and their familiarity with a range of poems that they could read with children. In order to select appropriate poems as models for children to use, teachers need to be familiar with a wide range of poems themselves. The other key issue was the approach to poetry teaching. Most students' experience of poetry teaching from their own education was very dry and often consisted of deconstructing poems line by line. The use of dialogic teaching enabled students to discuss poems and poetic language without the fear of 'being wrong' and allowed them to learn from each other, building on the contributions of their peers. This was one of the significant findings from the project.

Figure 2.4 Using paint charts to encourage adventurous use of colour vocabulary

When assessing any written work that has been completed as part of a cross-curricular science and English activity it is important to view it from two perspectives: (1) assessing the language features, and (2) the scientific content. When assessing it from an English point of view it is important to focus on the features of the genre selected as well as sentence structure and use of connectives. For science you would focus on the content knowledge and the science-specific vocabulary. Jackson et al. (2010) carried out a combined poetry and science activity investigating rocks. As part of the study, they devised a set of rules for assessing the children's poems which consisted of three strands: science content knowledge, sensory images and use of language. This ensures that the outcome of the joint cross-curricular project has served to develop the children's learning in both subjects.

As can be seen, working with English and science in a cross-curricular way has the potential to enhance children's learning in both subjects. In English, children can develop specific comprehension skills associated with non-fiction texts, the composition of non-fiction texts, and speaking and listening skills – in particular, those associated with exploratory talk and group interaction. In science, both content knowledge and skills associated with investigation can be developed. However, it is vital that teachers carefully plan the learning sequence to ensure that the knowledge, skills and concepts are identified and subsequently developed. Simply reading, writing or talking in other curriculum areas is not enough to develop children's learning: specific objectives need to be identified and explicitly taught. If not, there is the danger that the activities might become mere time-fillers and 'low-grade topic work in which thematic serendipity counts for more than knowledge and skill' (Alexander, 2010: 266).

Task 2.1

Teachers are often concerned about providing good enough evidence of children's learning in science.

Do you think that the granite poem in Chapter 11 is sufficient evidence that children have observed carefully? Some children conducted and videoed an interview for a TV news programme explaining the recent findings made by their school's scientific research laboratory. Is this sufficient evidence to show that they can collect evidence which is trustworthy, or to demonstrate that they can present their findings?

Make a list of other ways English can support children in communicating their learning in science.

References

Agar, J., Jones, S. and Simpson, G. (1999) *Teaching Children to Generate Questions Designed to Improve their Capacity to Think Critically About Scientific Problems.* Available at http://www.ntrp.org.uk/sites/all/documents/Agar-Jones-Simpson%20-%20questions%20science%20-%201999.pdf [accessed 29 May 2012].

Alexander, R. (2008) *Towards Dialogic Teaching: Rethinking Classroom Talk.* Fourth edition. Thirsk: Dialogos.

Alexander, R. (ed.) (2010) *Children, their World, their Education: Final Report and Recommendations of the Cambridge Primary Review.* London: Routledge.

Anderson, L.W. and Krathwohl, D.R. (eds.) (2001) *A Taxonomy for Learning, Teaching and Assessing: A Revision of Bloom's Taxonomy of Educational Objectives.* London: Longman.

Corden, R. (2000) *Literacy and Learning Through Talk.* Buckingham: Open University Press.

Dawes, L. (2000) *Thinking Together*. Birmingham: Imaginative Minds.

DfE (2011) *The Framework for the National Curriculum: A Report by the Expert Panel for the National Curriculum Review*. London: Department for Education.

Galton, M., Hargreaves, L., Comber, C., Wall, D. and Pell, T. (1999) *Inside the Primary Classroom: 20 Years On*. London: Routledge.

Grugeon, E., Hubbard, L., Smith, C. and Dawes, L. (1999) *Teaching Speaking and Listening in the Primary School*. London: David Fulton.

Harlen, W. and Qualter, A. (2009) *The Teaching of Science in Primary Schools*. Fifth edition. London: David Fulton.

Hull, R. (2010) *Poetry From Reading to Writing: A Classroom Guide for Ages 7–11*. London: Routledge.

Jackson, J., Dickinson, G. and Horton, D. (2010) Rocks and rhymes! A geosciences activity combining field notes and poetry. *The Science Teacher*, 77(1): 27–31.

Johnston, J.S. (2009) What does the skill of observation look like in young children? *International Journal of Science Education* 31(18): 2511–25.

Loxley, P., Dawes, L., Nichols, L. and Dore, B. (2010) *Teaching Primary Science: Promoting Enjoyment and Developing Understanding*. Harlow: Pearson Education.

Mercer, N., Dawes, L., Wegerif, R. and Sams, C. (2004) Reasoning as a scientist: ways of helping children to use language to learn science. *British Educational Research Journal*, 30(3): 359–77.

Moore, S. and Moore, D. (1989) Literacy through content: content through literacy. *The Reading Teacher*, 42(3): 170–1.

National Reading Panel (2000) *Teaching Children to Read: An Evidence-based Assessment of the Scientific Research Literature on Reading and Its Implications for Reading Instruction*. Rockville, MD: NICHD. Available at http://www.nichd.nih.gov/publications/nrp/report.cfm [accessed 29 May 2012].

Neate, B. (1992) *Finding Out About Finding Out: A Practical Guide to Children's Information Books*. Sevenoaks: Hodder & Stoughton.

Neate, B. (2000) *The Writing Classroom*. London: David Fulton.

Palmer, S. and Corbett, P. (2003) *Literacy: What Works?* Cheltenham: Nelson Thorne.

Primary National Strategy (2006) *Developing Reading Comprehension*. London: HMSO.

Riley, J. (2000) *Developing Writing for Different Purposes: Teaching about Genre in the Early Years*. London: Paul Chapman Publishing.

Sweet, A.P. and Snow, C.E. (2003) *Rethinking Reading Comprehension*. New York: Guildford Press.

Thomson, A. (2011) *The MASQ project: making and asking science questions through application of Bloom's taxonomy*. Available at http://www.teachfind.com/national-strategies/masq-project-making-and-asking-science-questions-through-application-blooms-taxo [accessed 29 May 2012].

Wray, D. and Lewis, M. (1997) *Extending Literacy: Children Reading and Writing Non-Fiction*. London: Routledge.

Wray, D. (2006) *Teaching Literacy Across the Primary Curriculum*. Exeter: Learning Matters.

Poetry referred to:

Magee, W., *What is the Sun?*, published in Corbett, P. (2006) *The Works, Key Stage 1: Every Kind of Poem You Will Ever Need for the Literacy Hour*. London: Macmillan Children's Books.

McGough, R., *Haiku*, published in Cookson, P. (2000) *The Works: Every Kind of Poem You Will Ever Need for the Literacy Hour*. London: Macmillan Children's Books.

McGough, R., *The Reader of this Poem*, published in Patten, B. (ed.) (1999) *The Puffin Book of Utterly Brilliant Poetry*. London: Puffin.

Sackett, A. M., *Estuary*, published in Cookson, P. (2000) *The Works: Every Kind of Poem You Will Ever Need for the Literacy Hour*. London: Macmillan Children's Books.

3   Mathematics enhancing science

Shelagh Hendry

Why should mathematics, a subject that primary practitioners frequently see as discrete, be combined with any other subject in cross-curricular teaching and learning? And why should the most appropriate subject for that combination be science?

Sir Harold Kroto, writing in *The Independent* (12 May 2011), described science thus:

> it is the only philosophical construct devised by mankind to determine with any degree of reliability what is true, can be true and, most importantly, cannot be true ... Truth assumes that an experiment always behaves in the same way and no mystical entity tampers with the observation.
>
> (Kroto, 2011)

Throughout the science curriculum for schools, scientific enquiry engages a developing understanding of scientific knowledge with this 'truth' of investigation. The increasing expectation of accuracy and precision, alongside the recognition of why these elements are so significant in truthful observation, mean that mathematics and science become inextricable. Recording measurements derived from both simple and more complex instruments, and the data related to experiments, is central to the scientific process when predictions are tested against actual outcomes, and this frequently leads to the consideration of additional or more detailed measuring to clarify data analysis and eliminate possible errors.

At the same time, teachers of primary mathematics often find that children are struggling to make sense of their mathematics when applying specific skills which have been extensively taught – despite substantial research evidence suggesting that context and application of mathematics is vital for children to develop as mathematicians. This chapter focuses on the close connection between scientific enquiry and the application of practical mathematics skills (something many teachers are aware of, but exploit less often than perhaps they could), especially, but not exclusively, measurement, all points of the data-handling cycle and the conversion of units of measure for real purposes. It will focus particularly on plants and environmental studies across both Key Stages, with some suggested opportunities for specific activities, as a 'context'. This follows the emphasis in Realistic Mathematics Education (RME), developed in the Netherlands, on real world situations with active participation as a key to unlocking individual and group mathematical learning (Treffers and Beishuizen, 1999).

Numbers rule the universe

In the ultimate intermingling of science and mathematics, theoretical physics uses the language of mathematics to explain our world when no other language works as well: a seemingly simple indication is Einstein's famous formula e $= mc^2$. In a less simple situation, equations relating to quantum theory can cover several sheets of paper. As Pythagoras is credited with observing, numbers rule the universe.

For younger children, numbers enable them to talk about their science, explaining their findings, so the beginnings of early counting are intrinsic to their understanding of the world, which they engage with as scientists. That world is full of numbers, large and small: the age of the Earth, the distance of the Earth from the sun, the speed of light, the size of a virus, the multiplication of bacteria, the Fibonacci sequence 0 1 1 2 3 5 8 13 ...

Fibonacci numbers have some close connections with patterns in nature; many (but not all) flowers and plants have Fibonacci sequence numbers of petals, seeds and leaves. Google provides plenty of ideas to pursue this further: Emily Gravett has written a delightful book, *The Rabbit Problem*, which provides a cross-curricular consideration of the reproduction of rabbits through the same Fibonacci sequence, and has many inventive ideas promoting linked mathematics and science activities for young children (Gravett, 2009).

One of the more difficult mathematical formulae that primary children are expected to engage with is: average speed = distance travelled divided by total time taken. This is more appropriately linked to science than the random concepts to which it often finds itself attached. Rather than men on bicycles, why not consider animals or children running, swimming or just growing over time by considering average speed – how quickly *do* we grow? Calculations may require units to be converted for clarity and manipulation – measure in centimetres, but alter to decimal fractions of a metre to allow division by time (or vice versa).

Fractions themselves appear naturally in science; we halve or quarter fruit and vegetables to explore seeds and structure. If each half or quarter contains one seed, we can explore how many seeds can be gathered from a given number of fruit. This can lead to considering the plant's capacity to reproduce, which can be explored through germination experiments – do plants with few seeds germinate more consistently than those with many? Is the average germination 50 per cent or higher? What would be the implications of 100 per cent germination of specific seeds? Could we imagine a world in which *all* seeds achieved 100 per cent germination?

In scientific enquiry at the primary level, the expectation is that children will reach the 'right' answer by generating accurate information, without teacher control impeding the independence of those young scientists in planning and collaborating. This implies and encourages lessons which begin as problems, not as sets of instructions. Differing outcomes can develop from a task managed and the same task directed. One teacher described two groups of children engaged in an outdoor problem. Each group was set the same problem, but in one case the teacher 'waited to see if help was needed – it wasn't, much', while in the other, the teacher 'wouldn't leave them alone', constantly suggesting actions and possibilities. Both groups completed the activity, but only the first could replicate their actions with confidence – the second disagreed about what had previously been done and could not even remember basic initial steps. In relation to the quality of independent science investigation by primary children, this may sound familiar.

In its subject-specific exemplification, Ofsted (2010) asserts that children should 'operate like scientists' and science lessons should be active. If children test ideas and generate testable questions, they must inevitably gather evidence, in search of patterns (or not), which is capable of replication; their observations, measurements, and the consequent data support the key scientific concept of evaluating the success of the test/experiment and the refining of the initial idea into a more scientific hypothesis.

In the beginning

Peter Kelly has written convincingly of the disjunction between mathematics for the classroom and mathematics in everyday life, and the impact this has on a child's mathematical beliefs. He suggests that mathematical learning will 'remain largely useless beyond school' unless the disjunction is addressed: 'To begin, we might offer children considerable experience in searching for mathematics and relationships in the world around them ... Such activities must go beyond simply making use of counting, measures and money in other contexts' (Kelly, 2002). Knowledge and understanding of the world at Foundation Stage is a rich context for those experiences.

Anything being observed for scientific discussion can probably be labelled and/or counted as part of that observation without losing the focus on knowledge and understanding of the world; trees or plants in the outdoor environment have differences and similarities to consider in their leaves, flowers, height, width, colour and texture. An intriguing activity to undertake with very young children is to 'adopt a tree'. Each child learns to identify their own tree, through using all their senses – for example, through touch and smell: with their eyes closed, they are asked to identify if the tree they are taken to touch is their own or another. The fact that their tree is labelled with a number, through counting how many exist in total, is simply another element of precise identification.

Counting can be undertaken while shelling peas or beans, listening to or looking at noises, birds, leaves under a given tree, daisies, butterflies, stones or plants, and is part of that curiosity about the world around them which defines emerging science; any of these can also be labelled with number names to support basic number recognition.

Sorting by 'type' develops mathematics language through science observation when that language may also be essential for science discussion – such as *greater, smaller, heavier, lighter,* alongside positional language such as *under* (for example minibeasts under stones). Weighing on a balance (and counting) stones, conkers, seeds, mud, fruit or vegetables grown can be part of the greater conversation about natural objects, their origins, purpose, and distinct identities, which also generates the vocabulary of early science and encourages the formulation of scientific questions. Even a child mirroring taking the register using simple data and mark-making leads towards tallying, which was one of the earliest ways of recording number and quantity, and is part of the bank of accurate methods of recording of data which older children will need for collecting information during science tests.

Measuring, too, begins in the Foundation Stage with height/length of themselves, others, plants, paths, flower beds, puddles at different times of day or during different weathers to consider but a few. This measuring occurs in non-standard units such as large cubes, bricks, hands, feet, canes, ribbons, and becomes the first step on the way to accurate measurement which will support working like a scientist and ensure that data obtained is exact. Foundation Stage food experiences will naturally deal with mathematics, as well as taste, texture, smell and sight, through quantity, shape and measuring.

Forest schools' work in Early Years makes much of the outdoor experiences which support very early science, ensuring an articulated curiosity in the natural world. Shelter building is a frequent element of this and combines mathematical questions of size (will it shelter one, two or three children?), balance and positional language, with concepts of appropriate materials, strength, flexibility and waterproofing even for our youngest children, without forcing connections.

A baby clinic or visiting baby prompts consideration of growth and human development, as well as variation, in part through mathematical activities such as use of scales and visual size comparison – for example, finding a sock to match a foot. Gestation and growth are themselves a source of fascination to very young children as well as being real examples of the need for patience in activities which occur over long periods of observation. Waiting for an egg to hatch (or seeds to germinate) involves time, prediction compared to reality, visual measuring versus actual measuring, and perhaps the use of timers for turn-taking, all of which engage mathematical concepts and language alongside the scientific, providing an understanding more relational than instrumental (Skemp, 1976).

Moving on and growing up

The National Curriculum statements on scientific enquiry stress the importance of collecting evidence when trying to answer a question, and mathematics is often the medium for that collection. Information processing skills such as clarifying, sorting for relevance, sequencing and comparing and contrasting, also apply in both subjects. Close to the beginning of the present National Curriculum is a little remembered section concerning key skills applicable throughout the whole curriculum which, no matter what specific changes may be made to the content, will remain relevant. One of six key skills is application of number through other National Curriculum subjects and real life 'in order to process data' and to explain any reasoning used (DfEE/QCA, 1999: 21). Another is problem-solving: 'All subjects provide pupils with opportunities to respond to the challenge of problems and to plan, test, modify and review the progress needed to achieve particular outcomes' (DfEE/QCA, 1999). It is no difficult leap to find a close affinity between these statements and those which occur in the sections on scientific enquiry. It is also important to be clear that combining mathematical and scientific skills and reasoning gives purpose to language development for all students, not just those with English as an additional language, through practical experience and usage.

What represents most effective practice is the clarity of connection between National Curriculum breadth of study statements in mathematics and science in teachers' planning: 'approximating and estimating more systematically in their work in mathematics' has clear linkage to reasoned prediction in science supporting more accurate observations; 'applying their measuring skills in a range of contexts' supports real purpose and increasing accuracy in science to ensure fair testing is fair, and that observed outcomes are the result of what has occurred, not the 'expected' result. When considering 'drawing inferences from data in practical activities, and recognising the difference between meaningful and misleading representations of data', teachers spend time creating mathematics activities to cover this area when practical science offers opportunities of real significance to children both for their primary science and their life beyond (DfEE/QCA, 1999: 74). Ben Goldacre (2008), throughout his book, *Bad Science*, is scathing about the capacity of many people to believe data because it is seen to be 'scientific' and therefore true – the reverse also being evident when very selectively chosen data claim to be truth. In the twenty-first century children will need to be more interrogative; the primary science classroom should be their starting point.

A class act or classification?

The growth of plants is one of the most common observations over time in the primary classroom but is sometimes repeated at different age groups. It is a vehicle for measurement, but to measure what? The possibilities are almost endless and can be selected, at least in part, through choices relating to mathematical maturity: area of leaf, height of main stem, spread of plant leaves, amount of water given, amount of light permitted, mass of soil given, ratio of grit to soil, time to grow to given height, time to germinate, quantity of seeds germinating, germination time in relation to size of seed or pot, appropriate temperature for growth or germination, comparison of any of the above in respect of two or more differing plants, and so on.

After clarification of the elements to be measured comes the choice of informal or formal measures. Are cubes, ribbons, paper strips, counters and so on appropriate to the children's abilities or are formal measuring elements more suitable? Is the measurement to be in particular units or to be converted into decimal fractions of a larger unit? Will a degree of rounding be acceptable, and what does that look like?

If measurements provide the data, how will it be recorded and how will it be linked to the concept of accuracy and fair testing or used to discern trends and patterns? What data will be collected and does it help answer what is being questioned? Might it answer additional questions, or raise others? How will that data be collected – by whom, when and with what? What type of graph is most appropriate to the investigation; which scales will be read; what represents sensible axes divisions; is conversion of measures to larger or smaller units needed to help with recording or to align the recording of various groups through conversion to common units, and can the best data recording system for the experiment be identified either before or after the experiment itself?

Moving outside the classroom raises questions within the environment. With eyes closed, explore the change in temperature when moving from sunshine to shadow, and consider why animals or plants may prefer one area to another; later, measure exact changes with a thermometer over time. If appropriate, develop this as a data-logging record through longer periods of time and consider whether your initial reasoning remains reasonable. Measuring the site, beds, ratio of compost to soil, leaf mould to grit/sand, water to soil, aspects of angles of sunlight, layout of plants or speed of growth can replicate in miniature the plant trials at national gardens such as Wisley in Surrey. These factors can also apply to decisions about the best site for a minibeast home or shelter. Wettest versus driest, warmest versus coldest, windiest versus calmest part of school grounds inform decisions about the most appropriate place for: composting; setting up a bird table; a seating area for the class at break time? The possibilities are limitless – the mathematical application of measuring and data analysis is clear.

Early sorting and identification develops into consideration of variation and interdependence, and outdoors supports the widest possible studies. In the classroom, 'types', whether of plant, minibeast or soil, are limited to what can be safely and humanely brought inside and, as that action in itself affects the possible outcomes, so Sir Harold Kroto's 'truth' is under question. It has become clear over the years that children taking Key Stage 2 science SATs had a very limited range of experiences of plants; questions on grasses, water plants or trees left many children confused and uncertain. Outside the classroom, 'types' are only limited by the extent of risk, as assessed by the teacher, of the environment in which they are found, and the activities planned. If lucky enough to have a local park, lake, canal or market garden within reach, the range can be even larger. As a Year 6 teacher, I once spent an invigorating afternoon with a class of children (and other adults) surveying a stretch of local canal, measuring water depths and temperatures, alongside recording the plant and animal life adjacent to the areas tested and collecting water samples for further investigation back in class. With managed risk, particularly in relation to water safety and infection, most children encountered an environment that was under their noses, yet previously had been barely seen, let alone considered.

Simply observing and recording the varieties of grass present on the school grounds can produce a wealth of data which can be developed into a possible experiment relating to questions raised, or it can lead to further data collection to clarify why, how, where and in relation to which minibeasts such variety exists. It can open out into exploring the proportion of one grass type to another, and possibly testable reasons for that ratio.

Ratio and proportion is one of the areas of mathematics most likely to cause concern to teachers and children, and yet it is directly relevant to some experiments relating to the natural world around us – in context, children cease to notice that this is difficult. Consider the ratio of soil to grit/sand for plant growth or for a minibeast's preferred 'home'; seed to mealworms for bird tables; a mix of feeds to support egg production for chickens; water to plant food for optimum growth of plants; specific kinds of foods for a healthy diet or sandwich; or the balance of juices mixed to create a healthy drink which also tastes acceptable.

Another standard experiment is to have a flower absorb colour to indicate absorption of water – a pretty effect, but underused in generating reasoning and questions. If we know the length of stem and quantity of water, and are timing the absorption, we can calculate millimetres per hour/day of absorption and therefore the transfer of millilitres per day from pot to plant (could we factor evaporation into this, ignore it or see a need to cover the pot?) and from here we can predict how long it would take for a larger plant. If we use a tree as our larger plant, we may have to convert measures. Given a time, we should be able to calculate the size of plant that would take this long to absorb colour from tip to base. Is a different ratio of colour to water absorbed more or less quickly, and could we find out? And, a favourite for children, does the shape of the container – cube, cylinder, and so on – make any difference? Most importantly, pupils begin to explain scientifically why any of this matters and to whom.

We can also consider hydration (osmosis) using dried pulses, leaving them to soak in a measured amount of water. Mathematically we can consider counting or estimating the number of pulses, timing, measuring the gain in mass, the increase in individual size or shape and the quantity of liquid before and after the experiment. Scientifically we can predict what will happen and try to explain why, we can use measures and data collected to find out if we were correct, and to generate further questions. Would further water be absorbed – is there a finite amount? What would happen differently if the container was covered or uncovered?

A class of Key Stage 1 children growing root vegetable tops such as carrot, swede, parsnip and potato in water trays engaged in prediction followed by measuring the height using paper strips, which were then checked against a metre rule. They also measured the water absorbed, by recording how much was put into the tray over a fixed number of days and subtracting the water remaining, then made comparisons of this data in relation to the real thing grown in soil. They compared observations, carefully recorded, and graphed their findings using pictograms. Initial surprise that any growth took place in the trays at all was soon replaced by detailed discussion of why the plants in soil took a greater time, and a far greater quantity of water before they achieved a comparable height, while the collapse of the tops' growth led to much speculation, all of which could have provided activities for the next stages of the exploration. At no time did they realize that they had engaged in some complicated mathematics. There was not an expectation of guessing which mathematics skills were to be used but they were not always directly told either. This can promote interesting evaluation questions rather than starters: what units are/should be used; what is an acceptable level of precision; how can we move towards more and more refined calibration of representation; what is the most appropriate representation to support clarification of outcomes? Communication and reasoning are integral elements of both the scientific and mathematical experience.

Getting a handle on data?

Sets of graphs can be used to compare different pictures created by similar data. Science questions and understanding can be located through studying these. At an initial level, the graphing of food in cupboards or fridges at home can be linked to a topic on healthy eating, comparing anonymous teachers, perhaps, rather than children. Graphs of food carousel displays at local supermarkets suggest real questions about nutritional value as opposed to prompts to purchase, and their special offers, too, bear comparison; if different supermarkets promote the same types of purchase, there are implications for trying to choose a healthy diet. As an observation over time, the offers promoted in one supermarket can be seen to have an equal impact on choices.

When creating their own graphical representation of test outcomes, a class can prepare a complete guide to better representation of data by evaluating and comparing their completed graphs, then apply their own rules to another scientific concept. Look critically at a range of graphs of different science experiments – can they answer our questions? If not, is it the graph type or data representation which could be changed, or is it a different practical investigation we need?

In considering the significance of links made between mathematics and science, it is valid to query with children, 'Remember when we did . . . in science, how did this mathematics apply?' Conversely, 'Remember when we did . . . in mathematics, how could it be useful for our science?' A challenge to older children might be to make a plant grow at a specified angle or follow a pathway, which enables them to assess the concept that plants 'lean' towards the light because it is a necessary support for growth, while applying mathematical ideas of angles and pathways. When considering the role of insects in pollination, an activity programming Bee-Bots to travel a variety of pathways between large illustrations of flowers is not only a useful revision of the science concepts, but again, a mathematical exercise in angles and possibilities. If the potential genetic mixes are also explored, and the outcomes predicted, it is moving the science into new areas of variation where flow charts might support and demonstrate all the possible outcomes.

A measure of understanding

'Dig for Victory' promotes history links alongside mathematics and science, and this outline contains only some of the ideas generated by Key Stage 2 class teachers and children. If the school has the possibility of outdoor allotment-style growing of vegetables, relate input to output per square metre or per pot. Consider the ratio and proportion of one crop to another; use measures of length for spacing; measure the length and mass of a range of final sizes of specimen vegetables to explore average sizes/yields; derive fractional splits of workload between the children. The science focus can be optimum growth conditions, germination, diversity, healthy eating or more specific to child-generated questions. Raised beds make soil more accessible for exploring moisture content but sunshine data, growing identical crops indoors in comparison to outdoors, comparing covered with uncovered crops (does the colour of the covering have any impact?), measuring rainfall and keeping temperature charts may eventually provide several years of data to assess the best choices for the ensuing year, and enable children to understand the longer-term needs of plants. Extended links through to cookery, based on old cookery books, can compare old forms of measures to metric; quantities needed for sharing can be predicted, and scaled up or down appropriately. The cost of fresh home-grown vegetables now and then can be compared to present day shop-bought alternatives, with the global footprint of purchased food in travel time/distance factored in; a database of taste tests can explore preferences.

'Where do the leaves go?' is a challenge to explore why leaves are not all over the school grounds by late spring when they covered much of the grounds by late autumn. The mathematical focus may include estimating how many leaves cover a given area. Can children devise a way to be more accurate? They could count how many are found in a small section and multiply up (but let them think of a way first!) At the same time, they can consider the different sizes and varieties: are they all from 'our' trees? Why? Their disappearance leads to consideration of decomposition in nature and the part played by microorganisms, the structure of soil, or perhaps the needs of minibeasts and insects for shelter and food, or even the activities of worms following the intriguing discovery of dead leaves partially pulled into the Earth. It can also link to distance travelled and so prompt work on windblown seeds or pollination.

A field study of plants or minibeasts can be undertaken by measuring a square metre of ground to investigate and collect data on plant or animal life. Use marking out the square as a measuring exercise, including judging right angles. Observation of the plant or animal life in the square, which might include counting and data-handling, will then prompt a question generated by the observers, which could be around adding something to the area, covering the area with horticultural fleece, black plastic or carpet offcuts for example, comparing one section to another, perhaps simply considering if extra watering will produce changes in the data. Ensure children are aware of the need not to damage the animal life directly – leave escape routes for minibeasts that prefer their original conditions – then predict how long it will take for the change to impact, and check. Will it take the same time to revert if your changes are reversed, and can we find out? What are the implications for the effects of human behaviour on the environment? If the square metre is divided into several parts for change investigations, fractions may be relevant or, collating the data received from all of them, model a presentation where the data is expressed fractionally, letting children do the bulk of the conversions.

In one class, 15 plots were selected for a class of 30, so a half was not a possible fraction. One-third of the 15 plots were excluding light (five plots) and of these, two-fifths had more woodlice than any other minibeast, three-fifths having other minibeasts in top position on their collection chart. The children reasoned that they could not say with any certainty whether excluding light encouraged or discouraged woodlice because the sample size was not large enough. Their solution was for all 15 plots to exclude light and count the woodlice. As ever, time intervened so they continued the testing through break and lunchtimes. If percentages need some rehearsal, here is a perfect opportunity when children are caught up in the enthusiasm of discovery and the mathematics fits naturally.

Relevance improves achievement, certainly engagement as exemplified in RME. Children need to understand why mathematics is important, to make sense of the purpose of different mathematics skills so they do not view these as 'boxed up'. They also need to develop an appreciation of why mathematics is such a significant part of the language and 'truth' of science. For the teacher, this requires clarity between the skills to be taught and the activities used to teach. In combining mathematics and science, additionally there is the recognition of which skills can be most effectively applied to which scientific enquiry. If we fail to identify the mathematics in science ourselves, small wonder that the children we teach also fail to spot the significance of the mathematics to their scientific enquiries.

Since 2009, when the Key Stage 2 science SAT was discontinued, many science subject leaders have reported a loss of status for primary science, particularly throughout Key Stage 2. Yet it remains a core subject which will continue to be an essential part of primary teaching and learning. Indeed, with the undoubted need for more rather than fewer scientists as we move through the twenty-first century, primary science should surely be an exciting and purposeful area of learning, and therefore the connection between it and the application of mathematical skills and knowledge is a powerful positive link. It is not a bolt-on, but part of a dynamic partnership that will increase confidence and clarity of learning in both areas at the expense of neither.

Task 3.1

This task considers progression and long-term planning.

Using your school allotment as a starting point in a topic 'Dig for Victory', focus on an Early Years class, a Year 2 class, Year 4 class and Year 6 class.

Think about the opportunities for learning about growth and plant cycles in each class. In outline, plan for progression in children's scientific knowledge. Then, using the suggestions in this chapter, plan for progression in mathematics.

References

DfEE/QCA (1999) *The National Curriculum Handbook for Primary Teachers in England*. London: Department for Education and Employment/Qualifications and Curriculum Authority.

Goldacre, B. (2008) *Bad Science*. London: Fourth Estate.

Gravett, E. (2009) *The Rabbit Problem*. London: Macmillan Children's Books.

Kelly, P. (2002) Does numeracy in school lead to numeracy out of school? *Mathematics Teaching*, 180: 37–9.

Kroto, H. (2011) Why Science teaching is an ethical issue. *The Independent*, 12 May 2011. Available at http://www.independent.co.uk/news/education/schools/why-science-teaching-is-an-educational-issue-2282636.html [accessed 29 May 2012].

Ofsted (2010) *Supplementary Subject-Specific Guidance for Science - Grade Descriptions: the quality of teaching in science*. Available at http://www.ofsted.gov.uk/resources/generic-grade-descriptors-and-supplementary-subject-specific-guidance-for-inspectors-making-judgemen   [accessed 29 May 2012].

Skemp, R. (1976) Relational understanding and instrumental understanding. *Mathematics Teaching*, 77: 20–6.
Treffers, A. and Beishuizen, M. (1999) Realistic mathematics education in the Netherlands, in I. Thompson (ed.) *Issues in Teaching Numeracy in Primary Schools*. Buckingham: Open University Press.

4 ICT enhancing science

Cliff Porter

Introduction

The principal goal of education is to create men and women who are capable of doing new things, not simply repeating what other generations have done.

Jean Piaget (1896–1980)

There are many reasons for using information and communication technology (ICT) when teaching science in primary schools. It can help to motivate children, address individual special needs and open up a wealth of interactive learning opportunities. Perhaps one of the most compelling reasons is to emphasize how school science relates to the technologies that children use outside school every day.

Science offers an ideal opportunity to show the application of ICT skills in realistic and meaningful contexts. 'Real life' scientists use ICT to gather and manipulate data, control processes, communicate ideas and research information. These activities can be mirrored in the teaching and learning of primary science and, in doing so, enrich the ICT curriculum. Additionally, the use of ICT provides opportunities to explore a wider range of teaching and learning strategies in the science curriculum.

This chapter will look in more detail at the rationale for using ICT in primary school science and suggest ways the technology can be used in the classroom. It will not attempt to provide user guides for the range of technologies described, or deal with the use of ICT as an administrative tool. In general, specific software or hardware will not be discussed because these are being developed so rapidly that any detail would quickly become outdated. Instead, the aim is to suggest some of the outcomes that ICT can help to deliver as part of a range of teaching and learning activities.

Why use ICT in primary science?

If we teach today as we taught yesterday, we rob our children of tomorrow.

John Dewey, education philosopher (1859–1952)

The use of ICT in science should be considered, like any other teaching and learning strategy, in relation to factors such as learning styles, gender, ethnic background and inclusion. Used effectively, ICT can help to:

- support good pedagogical practice
- achieve specific teaching and learning objectives
- enable children to achieve and learn more effectively than they could do otherwise.

The primary school science curriculum offers many opportunities to link with, and develop skills required by, the ICT curriculum. Knowledge, understanding and skills that can be delivered using science as a context include:

- gathering information from databases and internet sources
- preparing, presenting and sharing information
- considering the relevance, validity and accuracy of information
- using simulations
- exploring models.

The application of ICT in science gives the opportunity to develop ICT skills in a meaningful and productive manner. For example, scientists in industry or research use ICT as a tool to collect, manipulate, analyse and present information. In the classroom, analogous activities in science investigations include the use of dataloggers, spreadsheets and presentation software. Used effectively, to deliver defined learning outcomes and to support sound learning strategies, ICT can be a useful tool in the teaching and learning of primary science.

Increased motivation and attainment in science

Children live in a technology-rich environment. The internet, computers, television, mobile telephones and games consoles are part of their everyday experience. Using ICT in the classroom can help to encourage children to become more engaged with their classroom science. It can raise the status of school science and improve motivation, engagement, focus and quality of work (Newton and Rogers, 2001).

A review of the literature, performed by Cox et al. (2004) reported on the impact of using ICT in science:

> The use of ICT has a positive effect on many areas of attainment in science … Through the use of ICT, pupils have improved their

understanding of scientific concepts, developed problem-solving skills, been helped to hypothesise scientific relationships and processes, and improved their scientific reasoning and scientific explanations.

Assistive technologies to aid inclusion

Although I cannot move, and have to speak through a computer, in my mind I am free.
                                            Stephen Hawking, theoretical physicist

Assistive or adaptive technologies are those which help to maintain, increase, or improve the functional capabilities of individuals with special needs. They can help children to communicate more effectively and so be more able to demonstrate their achievements. Children are found to gain greater confidence in their abilities, which can have beneficial effects on self-esteem and personal relationships. As children gain greater control, they become more independent and responsible learners (Becta, 2003). Available technologies include:

- screen reader software to convert text to audible speech
- large key keyboards
- speech recognition software
- touch-sensitive screens and alternatives to a computer mouse.

The Royal National Institute of Blind People (RNIB) publish excellent information on assistive technologies on their website.

ICT applications in science

The use of ICT can provide excellent support for teaching and learning in primary school science, as well as enabling children to gain ICT skills in a meaningful context. Central to the use of ICT should be a consideration of the best way to deliver specific learning outcomes. If using ICT does not enhance learning, it should not be used.

The approach taken here is to describe the technology and suggest some possible applications that support the teaching and learning of specific science skills and aspects of scientific enquiry. It cannot be an exhaustive list of applications and does not attempt to suggest activities for all curriculum areas. Instead, it is intended to stimulate ideas that enable the use of ICT to be tailored to meet particular teaching and learning needs.

Teachers' use of ICT to prepare resources and present science ideas

Teachers and support staff can use word processors and presentation software to produce a great deal of support materials. The use of ICT helps to produce high-quality resources and also allows them to be more easily tailored to meet the needs of individual children or groups. This can include changing font size, style or colour to aid children with visual impairment. It also allows worksheets and support materials to be readily differentiated for children of different abilities.

Writing frames can easily be altered to accommodate different abilities and learning outcomes. A writing frame to encourage a structured approach to science enquiry may include sections such as:

- The question I am going to try and answer is..........
- The things I am going to keep the same are..........
- The one thing I am going to change is..........
- I will measure these things..........
- Here are my measurements..........
- Here is the answer to my question..........

Having these sections on a word processor document allows children to write in a space that is not constrained, as it would be on a printed worksheet. A static, printed writing frame may contain either large intimidating areas of white space or insufficient space for children to write all they want to. Additionally, using a word-processor document allows children to edit, check spelling and modify their writing following discussions of their investigation. This helps to encourage a reflective approach to learning.

ICT is also a valuable tool in the presentation of science ideas. Presentation software enables images and text to be presented using an interactive whiteboard (IWB). It also enables teachers to embed features such as weblinks and video clips into a single presentation. This is useful when viewing several different elements as they are all accessed through a single presentation. It reduces the need to interrupt the flow of the learning activities and avoids any problems of being unable to find video files or web pages.

An interactive whiteboard (IWB) is an excellent way of presenting information to the class. However, it should be remembered that it is a two-way medium. Children can be actively involved in using the IWB and should be encouraged to be participants in the activity, rather than passive recipients of information delivered through the IWB. There is a range of commercially available software packages that include interactive quizzes and games which use this aspect of interactive whiteboards.

In science enquiry, children can be encouraged to draw graphs and highlight information using the drawing and text options on an IWB. A simple task could be to add labels or highlight information on images, such as a photograph of a plant, projected onto the IWB. When investigating the thermal insulation of different materials, dataloggers can be used to produce a cooling curve on the IWB in real time. Children can be challenged to draw their predicted graphs on the IWB and see how well they match the actual cooling curve. Showing digital microscope images of the different materials can help children to discuss insulation properties in relation to a material's physical properties.

There is a wealth of good software for the IWB, including animations and simulations that can be used to replace science enquiries. However, teachers should consider these uses with caution. For example, an IWB simulation in which children choose different materials to complete an electrical circuit allows them to investigate electrical conductors. Using the IWB, rather than actually constructing circuits and testing conductors, means that children would have a less rich learning experience. Such simulations are good for revising and reinforcing learning. Their use to completely replace practical, hands-on investigations should be avoided.

Communicating ideas and showcasing work

ICT opens a wide range of opportunities for children to communicate. It can engage children and allow those who are normally reticent to express themselves.

In school, presentations, video, audio and images can readily be stored for viewing by the class and others with access to the school network. The school website or other networking websites can enable children to showcase their work to a wider audience.

Email, video conferencing and projects such as the BBC's 'World Class' provide opportunities to collaborate with schools locally or internationally. In addition to cultural and linguistic exchange, there are opportunities to do some excellent science. Collaborations could include sharing weather information from different locations when investigating the seasons or climate change. Comparing diet and daily activity can enrich topics looking at health and well-being. Presentations, images and video can easily be shared.

Producing coherent video can be somewhat tricky but it is much easier to record and edit good-quality audio. Relatively low-cost digital audio recorders are becoming more readily available and those with a built-in microphone are quite straightforward to use. Some devices contain a small loudspeaker, but if recordings are to be listened to by the whole class, external loudspeakers will be needed. Alternatively, files can be downloaded to a computer with loudspeakers connected for playback.

The strength of these hand-held recorders comes in the fact that they record audio in formats that can be downloaded onto a computer for editing and playback. This allows children to carry out interviews or make sound recordings over an extended period of time. Material can then be edited into a coherent narrative which can be made available for others to listen to as a 'podcast' via the school network or website. It is possible to produce high-quality recordings in this manner. Children can make recordings and compare sounds from different parts of the school as well as producing audio reports of their findings.

While it does take some time to record and edit this type of audio, teachers and classroom assistants may find it useful for creating audible instructions for children with poor reading or visual impairment. If suitable volunteers are available, recordings can be made in different languages for children with English as an additional language. Children with impaired hearing may benefit by listening to recorded information several times or by using the appropriate audio aids.

Of utmost importance when sharing children's work or communicating via the internet is the issue of safeguarding. In essence, personal information that could identify an individual, or contains private email addresses or other contact details, should not be shared. An effective mechanism should be in place for children to report any individuals who are bullying or making them feel uncomfortable. Permissions from parents or guardians should always be in place. Further guidance can be obtained from the booklet, *Advice on Child Internet Safety* (UKCCIS, 2012).

ICT for making observations and measurements during investigations

A key part of any science investigation is making observations and taking measurements. ICT provides a way of enhancing these activities, and opens up opportunities to make observations that would otherwise not be possible.

Recording observations and documenting activities using digital cameras

Digital cameras are readily available and becoming more affordable. They have the advantage of being able to view images immediately on a computer screen or interactive whiteboard. Only good images need be selected for further editing or printing. Digital images can easily be included in presentations and word-processed documents.

Digital images are excellent ways to record the results of investigations and to illustrate or explain practical activities. Cameras often come with software that allows images to be placed in a sequence to produce a slideshow. Some may allow text labels or audio commentaries to be added. Children can take photographs during an activity and produce a slideshow to explain what they have done. This can help to engage children with poor literacy skills and also provides excellent evidence of the children's work. Slideshows can also be used as the basis of teacher-produced materials to support written instructions.

Digital cameras can be used to record activities that take place over extended periods of time – for example, the germination of seedlings or the growth of mould on bread (Figure 4.1).

Investigating fine detail using a digital microscope

Inexpensive microscopes can plug directly into computers and produce images on screen or projected onto an interactive whiteboard. They typically have magnifications that are useful for looking at minibeasts and examining everyday objects in detail. For example, observing the fine structure of fabrics or different paper tissues can add to investigations into which materials are best at absorbing water. When observing living things,

    (a)   (b)   (c)

Figure 4.1 Time lapse images, taken over a period of five days, showing the growth of bread mould
Note: the mouldy bread should not be removed from its sealed container and must be disposed of according to safety guidelines.

details of skin, fingerprints, hair, flowers, leaves and samples of pond life are always fascinating to children. Digital microscopes are fairly robust and, once connected to a computer, reasonably easy for children to use independently. Usually, it is possible to obtain still digital images from the microscope and some may even have the ability to capture moving video images – great for investigating the movement of a snail, slug or worm.

Observations with video

The ability to record good-quality video is becoming increasingly less expensive. Hand-held video recorders, mobile telephones, and even some web cameras can give good results and are relatively easy to use. During children's investigations, video can capture rapidly changing situations for later analysis and lead to discussions on the accuracy and reliability of observations.

A good example is the reaction between carbonated cola drinks and mints (often called 'Coke and Mentos'). This investigation is an excellent way of looking at changing materials while also practising ICT skills to capture the event. When mints are dropped into a bottle of cola, it causes an immediate and violent production of froth, which escapes from the top of the bottle. The froth can quickly spurt to a height of several metres before subsiding as all the carbon dioxide gas is released from the cola. The maximum height that the froth reaches and the time it takes for the reaction to complete are difficult to accurately judge in real time. The reaction is rapid, lasting only a few seconds, and the height of the cola froth is constantly changing. Using a video camera to record the reaction allows it to be replayed and analysed back in the classroom (Figure 4.2). No editing skills are needed, as the aim is simply to review the reaction and make observations with greater accuracy than is possible while it is happening. Indeed, children's surprise and excitement during the activity is part of its impact and enjoyment. Children can investigate a range of factors, such as the number of mints added, the effects of different types of cola or mints, or the temperature of the cola.

Another use of video is in the investigation of motion. Children can be filmed as they walk, run, jog or skip to analyse how the body moves. The motion of a balloon-powered car across the classroom floor can be captured and slowed down to allow children to measure the distance moved and time taken, and then calculate its speed. The height a ball bounces when dropped on different surfaces, or from different heights, can be replayed and measured. Such analyses would be difficult and unreliable without the ability to replay and review the motion. Video can also be set up to show areas where children cannot easily access or where they

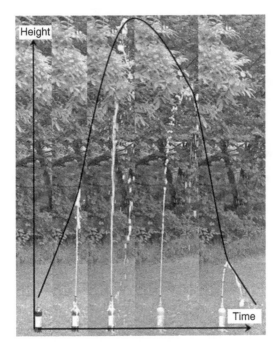

Figure 4.2 The reaction of cola and mints
Note: Children can enjoy the spectacle at the same time as it is captured on video. A graph of the reaction can be assembled using a sequence of stills taken from the video, or traced from the screen using a clear acetate.

would disturb the events being observed. For example, a video camera can record the activity of birds coming to and from a nesting box in the school grounds. Other than to place and retrieve the camera, activity can be observed without disturbing the birds. With more sophistication, a web camera could be set up to show the birds' activity on the school website.

As with all digital media, video can be stored and shared on the school network or for a wider audience on websites such as YouTube, as long as appropriate permissions and safeguards are taken into consideration.

Measuring with dataloggers

A range of devices are available to automatically record factors such as temperature, light intensity, movement or sound levels. Portable, hand-held dataloggers are useful for gathering data away from the classroom. Once measurements have been recorded by the datalogger, they are typically downloaded onto a computer for analysis and viewing. Most come with bespoke software and support packages to enable this to be done easily. Increasingly, dataloggers are being produced with built-in screens to view numerical data and simple graphs. These allow results to be shown immediately, but are limited by their size and their screens are only viewable by a small number of children at any one time.

One use of dataloggers is to take many readings in a short period of time, to capture rapidly changing events. A typical investigation might be looking at how the angle of a ramp influences the speed of a toy car rolling down it. Children cannot accurately measure the speed of the car on the ramp. To overcome this, the speed is often inferred by having children measure how far the car travels across the floor after it leaves the ramp. To interpret this, children need to make the conceptual connection between the distance the car travels on the floor and its speed on the ramp. A more direct approach would be to use a datalogger and two light gates to directly measure the speed of the car on the ramp.

Dataloggers can also be set to take readings over extended periods of time. This allows data to be recorded at times when children would be unable to take measurements. Children could predict the shape of a graph showing light intensity in the classroom over a 24-hour period and then use a datalogger to measure it. A motion sensor could be set up to measure the nocturnal activity of a pet gerbil. A weather station could take hourly readings of temperature and wind speed over several days to allow children to investigate the accuracy of weather forecasts from different media sources.

Although this does not use a datalogger to its full potential, most can be used in a 'meter' mode to take direct readings. Many hand-held dataloggers come with built-in probes for temperature, light and sound. Additional probes can extend the datalogger to measure other factors such as motion, air pressure, pulse rate, humidity or pH. Using a light sensor means that children can take readings of light intensity around the classroom. A good example can be found in Chapter 9, where children are investigating Ricky's sunglasses. A sound sensor can be used to investigate which materials would be the best for soundproofing a room, or to compare the levels of noise in the playground and classroom. Using dataloggers in this way gives children the opportunity to measure factors that they would otherwise find difficult to quantify. For younger children, just being able to measure and quantify sound can lead into many investigations on hearing. What is the quietest sound that can be heard? How does the distance from a sound source influence how loud it appears?

There is a temptation to only ever use dataloggers in their metering mode. This should be avoided. It is a waste of time using a datalogger to investigate the cooling of a liquid, if all that the children do is look at the screen each minute and write down the temperature it displays. The datalogger is capable of taking measurements automatically and producing a graph which shows the cooling. The children's time may then be used more profitably.

Analysing data trends and patterns using spreadsheets and graph software

Children's investigations in science can generate a great deal of information that needs to be sorted, analysed and presented. Using ICT to achieve this can help to engage children and enable them to produce high-quality presentations of their work. It also allows children to move quickly into asking searching questions and analysing their findings, rather than getting bogged down in the production of tables and graphs. In addition, work produced by ICT can easily be stored for later retrieval or more widely publicized on the school network or website.

Spreadsheets and graph-producing software allow mathematical operations to be performed and graphs to be drawn automatically. The use of spreadsheets helps to remove barriers for children with poor mathematical skills and speeds up the process of presenting investigation results. Spreadsheets and graph software enable children to move on quickly to considering more stretching 'what if' types of questions and seeing the outcomes. For example, what happens to the average height of the class if the teacher's height is included? How would the results be affected if certain children were absent and their heights not included in the results? Operations such as averages, additions, subtractions, divisions, multiplications and percentages can be preloaded into a spreadsheet. When children enter their own data, they immediately see it manipulated and presented graphically, and can quickly move to analysing the results of their investigations. Spreadsheets can be set up to give lines of best fit and children can produce their own spreadsheets. The figures below illustrate how investigation results can be manipulated and presented using spreadsheets.

A note of caution should be expressed here. If the learning outcome is for children to practice calculations or plot graphs, then the use of ICT in this instance may be inappropriate.

Children enter their heights into the spreadsheet. It has been set up to automatically calculate the average heights for boys, girls and the whole class. The bar chart changes as each result is put in (or removed) – see Figure 4.3. Children can predict the outcomes of actions such as what would happen to the average height for girls if Jeanne had been absent and her height not included? How much would this change the average height for the whole class?

Enter your height in metres

	Girls	Boys
Abi	1.20	
David		1.22
Gary		1.31
Grace	1.24	
James		1.22
Jeanne	1.16	
John		1.17
Joseph		1.21
Kurt		1.28
Mark		1.29
Miya	1.20	
Monica	1.19	
Naomi	1.18	
Niamh	1.22	
Omar		1.25
Pierre		1.24
Rachel	1.15	
Sean		1.18
Susan	1.20	

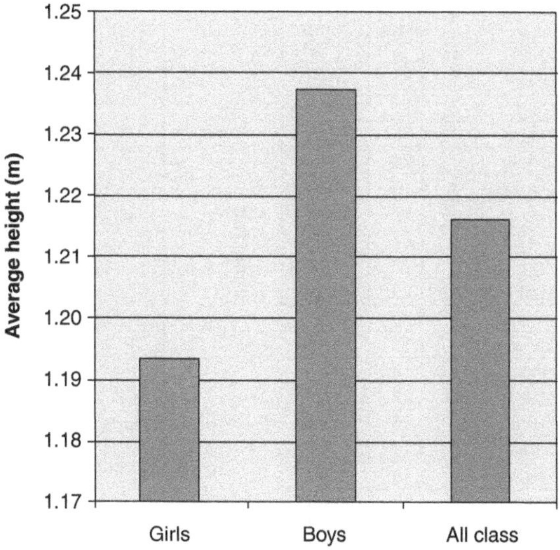

Average	Girls	Boys	All class
height (m)	1.19	1.24	1.22

Figure 4.3 Investigating class height

Children enter their heights and standing long jump measurements into the spreadsheet. A scattergram is automatically produced (Figure 4.4). A line of best fit can be added automatically if required.

Children enter the total number of seeds planted and the number that have germinated over a period of time. The graph plots automatically (Figure 4.5). Children can be asked to predict the shape of the graph as it emerges.

Using the internet to answer children's research questions

The internet holds a wealth of information and interactive resources, such as video clips, animations and simulations, for children to use. The skills required to consider the reliability and relevance of data from scientific investigations are also applicable when children consider information sources on the internet. Children should be encouraged to consider if information is repeated and consistent from several sources. Is the website

Enter your height in metres.
Enter how far you jumped in metres.

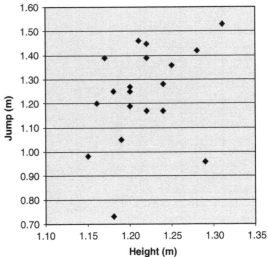

	Height	Jump
Abi	1.20	1.25
David	1.22	1.45
Gary	1.31	1.53
Grace	1.24	1.28
James	1.22	1.17
Jeanne	1.16	1.20
John	1.17	1.39
Joseph	1.21	1.46
Kurt	1.28	1.42
Mark	1.29	0.96
Miya	1.20	1.19
Monica	1.19	1.05
Naomi	1.18	0.73
Niamh	1.22	1.39
Omar	1.25	1.36
Pierre	1.24	1.17
Rachel	1.15	0.98
Sean	1.18	1.25
Susan	1.20	1.27

Figure 4.4 Do taller people jump further?

a private one or from an organization with a reputation to protect? Is the author giving a fair representation of the information or do they have a particular bias to promote? To guide children to specific sources, teachers can include web addresses in text documents and presentations. Children simply click on a link to navigate to the required web page.

Seed germination

Total number of seeds planted 158

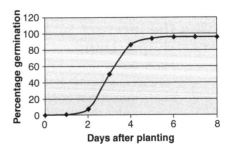

Day	Seeds germinated	% germination
0	0	0
1	1	1
2	12	8
3	79	50
4	136	86
5	149	94
6	151	96
7	151	96
8	151	96

Figure 4.5 How quickly do seeds germinate?

For the future

Computers themselves, and software yet to be developed, will revolutionize the way we learn.
Steve Jobs, co-founder of Apple Inc (1955–2011)

Smart phones, tablet computers and applications

Smart mobile telephones and tablet computers, with touch-sensitive screens, are widely available and even young children are likely to be familiar with them from their home life. The exciting thing about these devices is that, once their operation has been learned, they are easy to use and can be loaded with an increasing range of applications. The devices readily browse the internet, display documents and play video and audio. Interactive books are becoming available that will contain embedded multimedia and animations in their pages. These will enrich children's experiences of learning and, as with other assistive technologies, help to break down barriers to learning for those with particular needs.

Tablets and smart phones can have small programs, called applications, loaded onto them. The range of applications is increasing by the day. In effect, if you can imagine a use for a tablet computer, it is likely that someone will have written an application that is able to do it. Currently available applications include ones that allow a smart phone or tablet to act as a light meter, an interactive star map, movement sensor, sound meter, voice recorder, or to display weather data including rainfall radar maps and forecasts. Many have in-built wireless connectivity, internet and satellite navigation systems, which help them to be used outside the classroom. The use of tablet computers in education will only expand, and they have the possibility to greatly enrich teaching and learning in the science curriculum.

Gaming technologies in education

It is often said that children only have short attention spans. However, many will spend a great deal of time engaged in computer games or communicating through social networks. Clearly, children readily engage with virtual worlds and simulations. In a study looking at primary children's learning in geography, their achievement, motivation and engagement showed significant gains when participating in a game-based learning environment when compared to more traditional teaching methods (Tuzun et al., 2009). This suggests that such technology can be used, as part of a range of strategies, to support children's learning.

Challenges and opportunities

It is clear that the development of ICT, and other unforeseen technologies, will continue have a great impact on teaching and learning in the future. The challenge will be to make its use effective in advancing the learning of children with different aptitudes, motivations, learning styles and individual needs. Ensuring that the technology is integrated into successful strategies will still remain the job of the skilled classroom teacher and their support staff.

Task 4.1

From the range of ICT applications below, which support science as discussed in this chapter

- Spreadsheets
- Dataloggers
- Digital microscope
- Showcasing ideas
- Hand-held video
- Digital camera
- Simulations
- Communicating through emails; blogs

Identify those that you use confidently:

a) in your personal life
b) to support your teaching of science

and those that the children use as part of their learning.

Does the school have the necessary equipment, both software and hardware?
How often do the children decide when and how to use ICT?

References

Becta (2003) *What the Research Says About ICT Supporting Special Educational Needs (SEN) and Inclusion.* British Educational Communications and Technology Agency (Becta) ICT research report. Coventry: Becta. Available at: http://www.mmiweb.org.uk/publications/ict/Research_ SEN.pdf [accessed 29 May 2012].

Cox, M., Abbott, C., Webb, M., Blakeley, B., Beauchamp, T. and Rhodes, V. (2004) *ICT and Attainment: A Review of the Research Literature.* A report to the Department for Education and Science (DfES), ICT in Schools Research and Evaluation Series, No. 17. London: DfES: page 3. Available at: http://eec.edc.org/cwis_docs/Vivians/ict_ attainment_summary.pdf [accessed 29 May 2012].

Newton, L. and Rogers, L. (2001) *Teaching Science with ICT*, volume 1. London: Continuum International Publishing Group.

UKCCIS (2012) *Advice on Child Internet Safety.* The UK Council for Child Internet Safety. Available at: https://www.education.gov.uk/ publications/standard/Safegauardingchildren/Page1/DFE-00004-2012 [accessed 29 May 2012].

Tuzun, H., Yılmaz-Soyl, M., Karakus, T., Inal, Y. and Kızılkaya, G. (2009) The effects of computer games on primary school students' achievement and motivation in geography learning. *Computers and Education,* 52(1): 68–77.

5   Geography enhancing science

Arthur Kelly

Introduction

This chapter explores the distinctiveness, synergies and parallels between geography and science and how when, in particular circumstances, they are taught together they can produce powerful learning experiences for primary aged pupils. The chapter opens with an examination of curriculum matters and moves on to geography and its key concepts relating to understanding the planet we live on. It then discusses the links between science and geography, which as a subject has traditionally drawn upon scientific subject knowledge to develop understanding in relation to the key concepts, and using scientific methodology as part of the construction of knowledge. While Earth scientists may be interested in the physics and chemistry involved in plate tectonics and vulcanicity, geographers would go on to explore the spatial aspects of these physical processes and their potential human impacts and consequences. This robust relationship is outlined in the concluding part of the chapter, with a discussion of case studies relating to learning about weather and climate, and rocks, respectively. It is argued that the central question about cross-curricular as opposed to subject-led approaches should not be 'either/or' but 'when'. Teachers need to make sound professional judgements about this question based on their understanding of a diverse range of factors, not least their knowledge of the subject matter to be taught and their pupils.

Curriculum matters

The current primary National Curriculum framework for England (DfEE/ QCA, 1999) is organized into 'traditional' subject areas such as science and geography, which are familiar to most of us from our secondary school education. While our current National Curriculum is divided into subjects, other countries make different political choices regarding national curricula, some being values-led, others thematic, and some countries have no national curriculum at all. One does not even have to travel outside the British Isles to find different strategies regarding curriculum organization. Indications are that the current administration will also favour this subject-led approach. This would seem to suggest that these subjects should be taught in a discrete manner, yet subsequent curriculum guidance provided indicated that thematic or cross-curricular approaches could also be possible 'if **strong** enough links are created between subjects' (DfEE/QCA, 1999: 17).

The importance of strong links in cross-curricular approaches will be returned to below. So while the National Curriculum was grouped into subjects, schools were encouraged by the Government to innovate, take control of the curriculum and make their own decisions on how to teach (DfES, 2003). However, there was a perception that many schools did not follow this guidance.

The Independent Review of the Primary Curriculum (Rose, 2009) suggested a radical re-visioning of the primary curriculum from the discrete subjects of Curriculum 2000 to six areas of learning, more in line with the Foundation Stage curriculum (DCSF, 2008). One of the justifications for the review was to try and reduce the curriculum overload of an overly proscribed curriculum to meet the learning needs of pupils more effectively (Rose, 2009). Under these recommendations, science would have been taught as an aspect of scientific and technological understanding and geography through historical, geographical and social understanding. It is also notable that the review did not totally distance itself from subject teaching in promoting cross-curricular approaches:

> Our primary schools also show that high standards are best secured when essential knowledge and skills are learned both through direct, high-quality subject teaching and also through this content being applied and used in cross-curricular studies.
>
> (Rose, 2009: 2)

While this proposed curriculum had a number of strengths and limitations (Coe, 2010; Hayes, 2010), it never became a reality as a change of government in 2010 led to the shelving of these proposals and a further review of the primary curriculum (DfE, 2010) with consultation on the shape of the new curriculum (DfE, 2011b). While the status of *knowledge* seems to have increased (see below) and 'traditional' subjects as opposed to themes, the following is of relevance:

> There are a number of components of a broad and balanced school curriculum that should be developed on the basis of local or school-level decision making, rather than prescribed national Programmes of Study. To facilitate this, the National Curriculum

should not absorb the overwhelming majority of teaching time in schools.

(DfE, 2011b: 6)

This seems to imply that schools will have more freedom in curriculum design, thus providing space for a 'mixed economy' of approaches. Having explored a number of aspects of the curriculum, the chapter now moves on to an exploration of the distinctiveness of geography.

The distinctiveness of the geographical view

What, then, is the geographical view? The word geography comes from the Greek words Geo ($\gamma\eta$) or Gaea ($\gamma\alpha\iota\alpha$), both meaning 'Earth', and graphein ($\gamma\rho\alpha\varphi\varepsilon\iota\nu$) meaning 'to describe' or 'to write' or 'to map'. Geography is a diverse discipline that seeks to understand the Earth and all of its human and natural complexities – not merely where objects are, but how they have changed and come to be. Kant identified geography and history as the two basic forms of human knowledge, the study of the spatial and the temporal, and Bonnett (2008) describes geography as 'one of humanity's big ideas' (Bonnett, 2008: 1). It is interesting that both Matthews and Herbert (2008) and Roberts (2003) quote a stanza from T.S. Eliot in defining what the essence of geography is:

> We shall not cease from exploration
> And the end of all our exploring
> Will be to arrive where we started
> And know the place for the first time

There is obviously a historical link between voyages of exploration, geography and science. The voyage of the Beagle was a scientific voyage of exploration, the most famous outcome of which was Darwin's *Origin of Species*, but there was also a range of lesser known work. For example, Captain (later Admiral) Fitzroy was a pioneering meteorologist paving the way for modern weather forecasting, who was awarded the gold medal of the Royal Geographical Society for his contributions. More recently, the Apollo missions have been amazing voyages of scientific discovery, which have also led to increased understanding of our own planet. Images of Earthrise from the lunar surface and Aldrin's description of the 'magnificent desolation' of the moon's surface heightened awareness of the fragility of the planet we live on.

Moving beyond these deeper meanings, it is possible to identify core geographical knowledge, concepts and skills. Subject knowledge is emphasized in the White Paper, 'The Importance of Teaching' (DfE, 2010) and the report of the Expert Panel to the Primary Curriculum Review (DfE, 2011b), leading to a debate about what constitutes geographical knowledge (Martin and Owens, 2011; Kinder and Lambert, 2012; Morgan, 2012). This has led to a concern that the geography curriculum should not become just an accumulation of facts relating to countries, capitals, and so on without a context. This spatial/locational framework is an important part of learning but not the only one. Kinder and Lambert (2012) make the analogy with learning a language – they suggest that just accumulating facts is like learning a language just through developing vocabulary lists: 'you may know a lot of words but you still cannot speak the language. For that you need grammar ... The grammar of geography is in its ideas and concepts' (Kinder and Lambert, 2012: 94).

Matthews and Herbert (2008) suggest that the core concepts of the subject are:

- space
- place
- environment.

This is not an uncontested area – the nature of geography, what constitutes geographical thinking, is a contentious field and definitions vary temporally and with authors. Golledge (2002) identifies 19 different key concepts underpinning geographical thinking. However, at a primary level there is a need for focus, and Catling (2010) suggests that understanding of:

- place
- natural and human environments
- spatial organization

are key elements of primary geography, which shows a strong concordance with Matthews and Herbert. However there is a suggestion (Owens, 2011) that the core concepts may be extended to include:

- diversity
- interdependence
- human and physical processes
- scale.

A number of key skills are involved in developing geographical knowledge and understanding – these are the processes through which content is developed. It is also through these processes that many of the strong associations between science and geography become evident. Fieldwork, use of secondary sources such as maps at a variety of scales, satellite images, survey data, and so on all provide processes through which understandings of the world can be developed. A key communication tool of geographers is the map, through which information is organized spatially and which allows interconnections and relationships to be deduced.

This section set out the distinctiveness of the geographic view and now the relationship between geography and science is explored.

The interrelated nature of science and geography

As noted above, there are strong historical links between science and geography, although this would be a relevant point to re-emphasize that geography is not one subject but many subdisciplines using the key concepts and methodologies outlined above (Bonnett, 2008). For many years geographers followed scientific empirical methods, in an attempt to frame geography as an academic subject and gain recognition as a science. Thus, if one took a dictionary definition of science as 'knowledge gained by detailed observation by deduction of the laws governing changes and conditions and by testing these deductions by experiment' (Clark, 1998: 358), it is clear that many aspects of geography fit this description (for example vulcanicity, meteorology and fluvial geomorphology), others do not. While many geographers would be happy to be considered as scientists, others do not employ empirical methodologies in their exploration of the world and would not be comfortable with that label. It is not quite as simple as physical geography being a science and human geography not (many academic departments award BScs for physical geography degrees and BAs for human geography degrees) – the quantitative revolution (Matthews and Herbert, 2008) saw the employment of statistical empirical methodologies in aspects of human geography such as demographics and migration.

So while aspects of geography can be viewed as sciences others cannot, which is in line with the nature of geography as a subject of synthesis, drawing upon both the sciences and humanities to better understand the world we live in. The world is complex, diverse and changing – it spins on its axis just as the continents creep – and the subjects of geographical study are similar. Of course a further complicating factor is that the solely empirical nature of science has been challenged in some quarters. Geography may therefore be seen as providing a link between cognitive and affective understanding of the world and has both a deep and long-standing relationship with science. An important component of human and physical geographies is the notion of processes – the notion that, underpinning the world we observe and map, there are explanatory stories. It is a statement that the world is open to reason and empirical study.

Another important link between the subjects comes through research into primary pedagogy and the insights provided by constructivist theorists such as Piaget, Vygotsky, Ausubel and Bruner (see, for example, Alexander, 2010). There is a wealth of research into children's ideas in science (see Harlen and Qualter, 2009 or Driver, 2000) and research into children's geographies has developed in recent years (Scoffham, 1998; Catling, 2003). What links these approaches is an understanding that children are geographers and scientists before they enter the formal education system and that effective teaching should engage with their developing ideas. This research has important ramifications for the processes underpinning teaching and learning, indicating that knowledge and understanding cannot simply be delivered, and that learning should be seen as an active process where children learn concepts actively through the process of a subject. The idea of science and geography as a verb, an active process, as opposed to a noun, a thing (to be learned), again provides strong associations, and this will now be explored.

Skills links – processes curriculum

As will be clear from the points above, at the time of writing the nature of the primary curriculum is being revised in terms of structure and content. In the following sections reference is made to the current curriculum in an illustrative manner, to highlight aspects of good pedagogy or subject distinctiveness. While the curriculum landscape will change apace, the geology of good pedagogy is more measured.

Geographical education develops procedural knowledge which relates to:

- enquiry and exploration
- fieldwork
- processing and communicating geographical information.

These facilitate the development of geographical understanding (Lambert and Martin, 2012) and there are again strong parallels with science. To date, different versions of the National Curriculum science and geography statutory programmes of study (PoS) have begun with the skills basis, and this may be seen to be linked to the pedagogical approach outlined above. So in the current PoS for science the first attainment target (AT1) relates to scientific enquiry, which should be taught through the contexts of the knowledge bases of the curriculum (AT2–4). It is suggested that pupils should be taught about the importance of collecting evidence through observation and measurement and develop investigative skills relating to:

- planning
- obtaining and presenting evidence
- considering evidence and evaluating.

While there are differences between the programmes of study for Key Stages 1 and 2, the importance of the scientific process is clear. Similarly, the geography PoS for Key Stages 1 and 2 is based on the development of geographical enquiry and skills, and teachers:

> should ensure that geographical enquiry and skills are used when developing knowledge and understanding of places, patterns and processes, and environmental change and sustainable development.
>
> (DfE, 2011a:119)

Once again it is made clear that the content should be developed through the process. Geography should be based on exploring geographical questions, and through this develop a range of skills including the ability to collect, record and analyse evidence, drawing conclusions (Figure 5.1).

Through the enquiry process, geography may be seen to be related to data collection, and this provides another strong link with science (Table 5.1). This data may be of a quantitative nature, such as the measurement of rainfall or temperature or the construction of distance decay

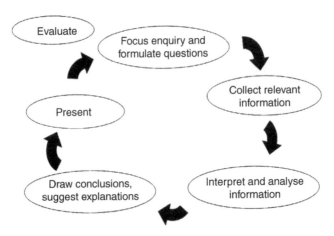

Figure 5.1 The process of geographical enquiry

Table 5.1 Geographical questions linked to key concepts

Geographical question	Geographical concept
Where is this place?	Location, scale
What is this place like?	Place, human and physical, environment, diversity
Why is this place as it is?	Human and physical processes
How is this place connected to other places?	Interdependence
How is this place changing?	Human and physical processes
What is it like to be in this place?	Place
How is this place similar to, or different from, another (MY) place?	Interdependence

curves in use of services. This empirical collection of quantitative data obviously has firm roots in scientific enquiry. Yet aspects of human geography make use of qualitative data, which may not be numerical and thus not 'scientific' in the traditional empirical sense. One of the geographical questions it is suggested that pupils investigate is 'What would it feel like to be in this place?' (Foley and Janikoun, 1996), which clearly links to the affective dimension and is not readily open to quantification. In fact the notion of place, which is at the centre of primary enquiry, has subjectivity at its heart:

The unique quality of place is that it goes beyond the objective and has affective meanings ... Place embodies the harmony of a defined territory and the meanings and experiences that are attached to it ... [it] catches the very basis of geography around which we build our lives.

(Matthews and Herbert, 2004: 165)

It is possible to argue that data collection in all forms can be seen to be scientific if the enquiry has rigour in analysing and drawing conclusions from evidence. While it is possible to identify commonalities between the enquiry/skills approaches, it is also important to note the divergences. So, in primary geography, pupils are encouraged to identify their *views* about places and those that others hold, including views on current topical issues. This flags up an important aspect of geography as a subject in which a multiplicity of views coexist, although it may be a naive view of science that does not see the same.

Having examined the parallels in scientific and geographic process, we now move to content and explore two areas where there are 'strong bonds' that could lead to successful cross-curricular learning.

Content links – knowledge curriculum

The aim of this section is to explore two areas, geology and meteorology, which lend themselves to geoscientific cross-curricular learning. That does not mean that these are the only two, and it will be for the reader to make their own judgements about further 'strong bonds' where the two subjects provide rich learning opportunities but would also allow development of knowledge, skills and understanding in English, mathematics and ICT. The main emphasis will be on looking at these themes from a geographical perspective, although reference will also be made to science.

Meteorology: weather and climate

> Meteorology encompasses the essence of geographical study … Studying weather and climate offers diverse opportunities to develop primary pupils' understanding of aspects of human and physical geography
>
> (Fordham, 2011: 14)

The study of weather and developing understanding of climate offers an excellent example of the relationship between geography and science. Obviously, teachers have to grasp the distinction between weather (the air, temperature, wind and precipitation that we directly experience) and climate (average conditions over a long time period). Table 5.2 highlights complementary process skills – weather study offers opportunities to develop these skills.

Table 5.2 Science and geography skills developed through the study of weather

Science skills	Geography skills
Key Stage 1	**Key Stage 1**
Ask questions	Ask geographical questions
Make and record observations and	Develop geographical vocabulary
measurements	Observe and record
Key Stage 2	**Key Stage 2**
Ask questions that can be investigated	Ask geographical questions
scientifically	
Make systematic observations and measurements	Collect and record evidence
Use observations, measurements or other data to	Analyse evidence and draw conclusions
draw conclusions	

Obvious key distinctions between the two domains here would be an understanding of what it means to investigate something scientifically, what *geographical* questions are, as opposed to scientific ones, and geography's interest in the global as well as the local. When investigating weather locally children are being scientists, but it could be argued that when they study weather in contrasting localities they are being geographers. The Meteorological Office (http://www.metoffice.gov.uk/education) provides a range of resources that could be used to support teaching and learning about weather and climate. Within these materials it is interesting to note that the 'scientific' ones relate to using thermometers to measure temperature and the mechanics of the water cycle, while the geographical ones focus on linking human activity to weather in different localities around the world and in specific mountain environments. Scientists would primarily be interested in the *physical processes* underpinning weather and climate, whereas the geographer would also be interested in the *human impact* of weather and climate (from how we feel about the weather today to the impact of a hurricane), the *diversity* of global weather and climate, and also *interdependence*, notably with respect to climate change. The Weather Club, a registered charity, has a website which provides a range of topical ideas to support teaching and learning about weather, and is a useful source.

Geographers would also be interested in the relationship between weather, climate and landscape. Developing understanding of world climate zones would enable pupils to describe the climate and landscapes of different parts of the world and also compare them. At upper Key Stage 2 they could also learn about geographic patterns in relation to climate zones and landscapes, using maps as well as the physical processes that underpin these. From a scientific perspective, this would include developing knowledge and understanding relating to the tilt of the Earth and circulation systems. From a geographical perspective, the description and comparison of, for example, polar, tropical and desert landscapes alongside an examination of climate data for those zones could develop key concepts relating to *place, diversity* and the importance of *location*.

Having established the existence of different climate zones, pupils could then explore climate change, which has obvious geographic and scientific links. From the scientific perspective this would include examination of climate data over time to draw conclusions. The evidence seems to suggest that there is a clear trend towards global warming, though the mechanisms underpinning this and its relationship to global extreme weather observed recently remain subject to some debate (Fordham, 2011). For the geographer, the key consideration would be the human and environmental impact – writing on the Arctic as a unique and fragile environment, Dunn et al. (2011: 19) observe, 'We should care about the loss of Arctic environments and the loss of biodiversity ... because these could affect all of us'.

Again, the key geographical concepts of diversity, interdependence and physical/human processes are highlighted. This global exploration of habitats could also be reinforced by developing more local understandings. It is very common for primary pupils to be involved in studying habitats within the school grounds, for example through the study of invertebrates ('minibeasts'). This provides another very good example of the strong bond between science and geography. Observation, prediction and inference combine with spatiality to deepen understanding. It is recognized that probably the most important factor shaping habitats is climate, and at a local level this may be evident through microclimate, so within the school grounds some species will be adapted to particular habitats – for example, woodlice are adapted to dark, damp places. In the study of habitats, concepts such as food chains and food webs are important to both geographers and scientists in developing deeper understanding, and provide a further example of how scientific understanding is at once informing and being informed by geographical understanding. This may also be seen through the instance of geographers' interest in landscape.

The study of landscape and its links with sense of place and regional or national identities has a long tradition in geography (Matthews and Herbert, 2004) and landscapes provide a further excellent example of the strong links between science and geography. While it is recognized that landscapes are formed through a dynamic interaction between physical factors and the human footprint, science, through knowledge and understanding of physical processes such as weathering, erosion and deposition, enhances geographical understanding. This allows geographers to go beyond describing landscapes to classify, compare and make generalizations. A scientific understanding of the chemical properties of limestone allows the connection to be made between the landscapes of the Yorkshire Dales and the Guilin Hills in China with the fact that limestone rocks dissolve to form Karst landscapes and cave systems. The study of landscape in geography can take place at a global (polar, desert, mountain, coastal) or local level. The process of physical weathering, and in particular freeze–thaw, can be introduced to primary aged pupils but this is obviously built on scientific understanding of physical changes of state. Water, in its liquid form, invades cracks in rocks but when the temperature falls below 0°C the water freezes, changes state to solid and expands by 10 per cent. This causes immense pressure on the surrounding rock, and over time this cycle of freezing and thawing can lead to the break-up of the rock, with resulting erosion and deposition. The process of freeze–thaw is one that will impact on the local area – in February 2011 the Government provided local authorities with an additional £100 million to deal with additional potholes caused by freezing conditions (BBC, 2011). Geographical field-work in the locality can also provide pupils with real contexts for the study of water, glacial and (to a lesser extent) wind erosion and how these physical processes are involved in shaping the landscape. The Earth Science Education Unit also provides examples of how these physical processes can be modelled in the classroom.

Geology: rocks

Another theme where the strong bonds between science and geography could be explored is through teaching and learning about rocks and soils. Similar links between scientific and geographic skills could be drawn as in the previous section. In terms of scientific skills, pupils could use observations to classify different rock types, for example igneous, sedimentary, metamorphic, and then use a dichotomous key to identify particular types (for instance, granite, sandstone, gneiss) and draw conclusions (Figures 5.2 and 5.3). Scientists may also be interested in the uses of these materials and how they relate to their properties. Geographers would be interested in where particular samples were found (*location*) and mapping them to develop understanding. Geographic enquiry would link to how the geology of particular locations impacts on the landscape and geography of that place. The red sandstones of the Cheshire plain have an important impact on the human geography of Merseyside (where I currently work) in terms of its utility as a building material, yet the chalk of Downland Kent (where I grew up) does not. These geographical observations must then go back to science to discover why, but it flags up how geographers would be interested in how the natural materials have been used by people.

Figure 5.2 Looking closely at granite

Figure 5.3 Children using observation to make a dichotomous key to identify particular types of rock

Older primary pupils could be challenged to learn about the structure and dynamism of the Earth. Secondary sources relating to planetary anatomy in terms of core, mantle and crust could be used to develop scientific and geographic understanding. Plotting earthquake boundaries and volcanic hotspots on a world map are a way of scaffolding observations of geographic patterns and then stimulating responses as to why these exist. The BBC have been responsible for some fantastic programmes (for example *Planet Earth, How the Earth Made Us*) and associated resources which would enable pupils to visualize and experience the awe and wonder associated with the planet we live on. Primary pupils can be introduced to plate tectonics and how the way they change the planet can be both slow and rapid (Halocha and Hawkins, 2011). There is a long-standing interest in geography relating to extreme natural events and the impact they have on people and places. The Japanese earthquake and tsunami of 2011 are examples of how such extreme events can be used to support developing understanding of geographical concepts, in terms of location (where the event occurred), physical geography (what mechanisms caused the event), human geography (what impact did it have on people? how are they rebuilding their lives?), environment (potential nuclear contamination at Fukushima) and interdependence (how can we help?).

An excellent source of support relating to bringing geology into the primary classroom is the Earth Science Education Unit website, which also offers free continuing professional development (CPD) for primary schools. If the preceding examples cause you to ponder 'where does the scientist stop and the geographer begin?', then perhaps that highlights the strong relationship between the two subjects.

Limitations of linking geography and science

The preceding discussion has clearly identified the strengths of teaching science and geography as part of a cross-curricular approach, but teachers should also be mindful of the limitations of such approaches. For some the 'Holy Grail' of cross-curricular approaches can potentially be a poisoned chalice (Hayes, 2010: 381). One of the key concerns is that interdisciplinary approaches can lead to a lack of rigour, both conceptually and in terms of skills development. Opponents cite colouring, copying and tracing of 'projects' in the 1970s as evidence of lack of rigour. Colouring in maps and graphs is not good science or good geography. There can also be a lack of rigour when links between subjects in a theme are tenuous rather than strong. I can remember some very weak links in my planning in the early days of my career when planning was thematic. Another concern relates to teachers' subject knowledge – it is often said that to be creative one needs to think 'outside of the box', but it may be argued that to do this one has to know what is in the box in the first place! By this I mean that in order to plan in a cross-curricular manner and make effective links, one needs to know what constitutes the key concepts, knowledge and skills within and between both subjects. Lack of understanding of this point can lead to lack of rigour in terms of skills and concept development. Coe (2010) appears to question the 'readiness' of teachers to move towards cross-curricular approaches:

> This will not be easy after 20 years of being cast as technicians who are required to deliver pre-packaged instruction. Having been trained to do this since the introduction of National Strategies in 1998, many teachers find themselves unprepared for the necessary flexibility to adjust in matching and carrying forward the responses of children
>
> (Coe, 2010: 401)

Hayes (2010) notes that cross-curricular teaching can be challenging for teachers in that it may flag up limitations in their knowledge and understanding. A further argument against cross-curricular work which embodies pupil choice is that it may lead to them avoid skills or concepts that they find hard (Hayes, 2010) although the current lack of physicists and mathematicians at post-16 level suggests that this issue is also present in a subject-led curriculum.

Conclusion

This chapter has explored the links between science and geography as disciplines and also explored some of the distinctiveness of the geographical world view. There are obvious 'strong bonds' between science and geography, and these interdisciplinary links would allow for similarly robust and rigorous cross-curricular approaches. The advantages of these cross-curricular approaches are evident, not least in terms of pedagogy, as are their potential limitations. At their best, cross-curricular approaches allow pupils to learn in a pedagogically appropriate, meaningful and intellectually rigorous manner. At their worst, they can lack learning challenge and provide a patchwork tour approach which lacks conceptual rigour and challenge. Ultimately, any curriculum is an artificial construct and the real world does not exist in these boxes – they may be thought of as lenses with which to view the world, each providing a particular perspective. Teachers need to be able to distinguish between curriculum as conceived at a national level and how it is organized in their schools and classrooms. The key question about cross-curricular as opposed to subject-led approaches is not 'either/or' but 'when'. Teachers need to make sound professional judgements about this question based on their understanding of a diverse range of factors, not least their knowledge of the 'subject' to be taught and their pupils. With the suggested increased freedoms for teachers to become curriculum architects rather than delivery operatives, this ability assumes central importance. The key factor underpinning this choice must always be: are pupils progressing, for what is any curriculum worth if they are not?

Task 5.1

The author has made the point that there are strong bonds between geography and science, but also stresses that we need to be aware of the distinctiveness of each subject.

Taking habitats as your context, identify:

a)   the science knowledge that children will learn
b)   the geography knowledge they will learn
c)   the science enquiry skills which will be developed
d)   the geography enquiry skills which will be developed.

References

Alexander, R. (ed.) (2010) *Children, their World, their Education: Final Report and Recommendations of the Cambridge Primary Review*. London: Routledge.

BBC (2011) *Potholes: Councils get extra £100m to fix winter damage*. Available from http://www.bbc.co.uk/news/uk-12546138 [accessed May 2012].

Bonnett, A. (2008) *What is Geography?* London: Sage.

Catling, S. (2003) Curriculum contested: primary geography and social justice. *Geography*, 88(3): 164–211.

Catling, S. (2010) Understanding and developing primary geography, in S. Scoffham (ed.) *Primary Geography Handbook*. Revised edition. Sheffield: Geographical Association: 74–93.

Clark, A. (1998) *Penguin Dictionary of Geography*. London: Penguin.

Coe, J. (2010) Areas of learning. *Education 3–13: International Journal of Primary, Elementary and Early Years Education*, 38(4): 395–402.

DCSF (2008) *Statutory Framework for the Early Years Foundation Stage*. Annesley: DCSF Publications.

DfE (2010) *The Importance of Teaching*. London: Department for Education.

DfE (2011a) *The National Curriculum for England: Geography*. London: Department for Education.

DfE (2011b) *The Framework for the National Curriculum: A Report by the Expert Panel for the National Curriculum Review*. London: Department for Education.

DfEE/QCA (1999) *The National Curriculum Handbook for Primary Teachers in England*. London: Department for Education and Employment/ Qualifications and Curriculum Authority.

DfES (2003) *Excellence and Enjoyment: A Strategy for Primary Schools*. London: DfES. Available at: http://webarchive.nationalarchives.gov .uk/20110202093118/ http:/nationalstrategies.standards.dcsf.gov.uk/ node/85287 [accessed 29 May 2012].

Driver, R. (2000) *Children's Ideas in Science*. Oxford: OUP.

Dunn, C., Johansson, M. and Callaghan, C. (2011) Arctic refrigerator overheating. *Primary Geography*, 76: 18–20.

Foley, M. and Janikoun, J. (1996) *The Really Practical Guide to Primary Geography*. Second edition. Cheltenham: Stanley Thornes.

Fordham, R. (2011) 2010: an extraordinary year for global weather. *Primary Geography*, 76: 14–15.

Golledge, R. (2002) The nature of geographic knowledge. *Annals of the Association of American Geographers*, 92: 1–14.

Halocha, J. and Hawkins, T. (2011) Changing fast, changing slow. *Primary Geography*, 76: 6–7.

Harlen, W. and Qualter, A. (2009) *The Teaching of Science in Primary Schools*. Fifth edition. London: David Fulton.

Hayes, D. (2010) The seductive charms of a cross-curricular approach. *Education 3–13: International Journal of Primary, Elementary and Early Years Education*, 38(4): 381–7.

Kinder, A. and Lambert, D. (2012) The National Curriculum Review: what geography should we teach? *Teaching Geography*, 36(3): 93–5.

Lambert, D. and Martin, F. (2012) Policy matters. *GA Magazine*, 20: 4–5.

Martin, F. and Owens, P. (2011) Well, what do you know? The forthcoming curriculum review. *Primary Geography*, 75: 28–9.

Matthews, J.A. and Herbert, D.T. (2004) *Unifying Geography: Common Heritage, Shared Future*. London: Routledge.

Matthews, J.A. and Herbert, D.T. (2008) *Geography: A Very Short Introduction*. Oxford: OUP.

Morgan, J. (2012) Knowledge and the school geography curriculum: a rough guide for teachers. *Teaching Geography*, 36(3): 93–5.

Owens, P. (2011) *Little Blue Planet: Investigating Spaceship Earth*. Sheffield: Geographical Association.

Roberts, M. (2003) *Learning Through Enquiry*. Sheffield: Geographical Association.

Rose, J. (2009) *Independent Review of the Primary Curriculum: Final Report*. London: DCSF. Available at https://www.education.gov.uk/publications/standard/publicationDetail/Page1/DCSF-00499-2009 [accessed 14 Feb 2012].

Scoffham, S. (ed.) (1998) *Primary Sources: Research Findings in Primary Geography*. Sheffield: Geographical Association.

Websites

Earth Sciences Education Unit: http://www.earthscienceeducation.com
The Weather Club: http://www.theweatherclub.org.uk

6   History enhancing science

Pat Hughes

Introduction

Sir Isaac Newton's statement (1675) that 'if he had seen further it is by standing on the shoulders of giants' illustrates the significance of history to science. Scientific knowledge develops by building on the work of earlier scientists. Historical knowledge opens a door to seeing science from a different age and can enhance the understanding of change, and also helps to ensure that science is linked to people. Making links between history and science offers the opportunity to broaden both knowledge and skills because key subject concepts such as investigation and change are covered in both subjects. Both scientists and historians ask questions, make hypotheses and look for and evaluate evidence. This chapter explores these links.

Last week, I visited the Neolithic site at Newgrange in Southern Ireland. Looking round the visitors' centre prior to our trip out to Newgrange by shuttle bus, Sam (aged 10) and I were fascinated by some pretty awful human teeth, from our Stone Age past, which had been found at the site. The little piece of paper underneath explained to us that these teeth were worn down by the type of food the people ate, in particular the flour used to make bread. As well as flour, it contained rough bits of the stone which had been used to grind the grain and consequently would chip the teeth. On the way home, we bought a white loaf to go with our chips and noted that we were unlikely to have chipped teeth as a result of eating this.

Bread and its major ingredient, flour, form part of our daily lives and this chapter suggests ways in which science in its broadest form can be used, together with history, to look at how one of the fundamental elements of our diet has changed and developed over the 5000-plus years since those Irish Neolithic teeth were ground down.

History can provide interesting starting points or a purposeful context in which to learn science. This chapter will start by looking at the types of bread that can be found easily today in a local supermarket, many of which will be familiar to children. Then it will look back to what those Neolithic teeth were chomping into. The long movement from then to now incorporates not just science but massive historical changes in the technology which produces the flour to make the bread. This aspect is touched on, but unless pupils have access to a working mill, either modern or historical, this is difficult to follow without seeing the machinery in service. Changes in the production of flour, and consequently in the bread we eat, also have an impact on diets, which leads to questions about what is added to bread, when these changes occurred and why.

What follows is a combination of traditional knowledge with experiential learning. Furedi (2009: 13) makes several important points about the 'infantilization of education', which is a direct result of challenges facing all adults in exercising authority. For teachers this can devalue the intellectual content of what is taught, as it has become negotiable with pupils. This is often, in terms of behaviour management, 'we behave, if you let us do . . .'.

Furedi claims the 'infantilization of education' produces an academic and social argument that sees knowledge as being unimportant, while the primary importance of what happens in school is the learning. The teacher's role is to facilitate this learning. This chapter does not take this line. It opens up the idea that there is some fundamental knowledge which pupils need to know and there are skills which can be acquired to support this learning. It also follows quite closely the ideas of Short et al. (1996) on providing a strong framework for supporting learners to engage in a 'process of searching for questions that are significant in their lives and finding multiple ways to examine and research those questions'. The major challenge, of course, is to work out how 'multiple ways' can be linked into a strong planning framework. Hopefully, this chapter provides some ways through doing this via cross-curricular links.

Investigating bread

A visit to any supermarket shows a huge array of flours and bread. Identifying some of these different breads could be a pre-theme homework task, and for some children will help to widen their horizons. They see that there is more than one sort of bread. It also helps to prepare children before they start investigating a topic in class (Hughes, 2008). Another useful starting point is an activity, *'the same but different'*, which can be used across the science curriculum. It encourages children to observe the different breads carefully. Children are shown a collection of different types of bread and are asked to choose two breads and say one thing which is the same about both types of bread and one thing that is different about them (Figure 6.1).

Figure 6.1 The same but different: choose two types of bread. How are they the same? How are they different?

Ideally, some preliminary tasting of different breads could take place as an outcome of this initial look at bread. This leads to the question 'What are the different breads made from?' The list of ingredients for white bread tells us that a particular loaf contains, among other things, wheat flour, water, yeast, salt, vegetable oil, and that it is suitable for vegetarians. A wholemeal loaf on the other hand contains wholemeal flour, wheatmeal flour and cracked wheat among other things. Ingredient labels of bread can make a useful study and display, and lead to questions such as 'What is cracked wheat?', and why certain ingredients, such as iron or some vitamins, are added to bread, and to exploring where such ingredients can be sourced. For the more serious bread specialist a list of ingredients illustrates the 'enriched' bread and flour content. In an economic crisis the percentage of the cheaper soya flour is increased to keep prices down. The need for children to be interested and involved in what they are eating is fundamental to their life chances. Collecting evidence about what is in bread through close observation, looking at the ingredients used to make bread, including additives, and tasting bread provides children with information which they can use to make choices about what they eat. It is also a fundamental life skill to question, inquire and discuss the purpose of ingredient labels for older primary children. Pupils should come up with their own questions, but 'framework' questions need to be identified if they are not asked spontaneously. Both older and younger pupils need to be encouraged and supported to examine exactly what does go into their mouths.

Bread in history: looking for and evaluating evidence

Archaeological evidence shows that it was not until people settled in one place that they started to grow some food themselves and cereals, including wheat, became key for making flour and bread. This leads to the questions, 'How do the archaeologists know that bread was eaten by Neolithic Man? What is the evidence for this?' In the Old Testament (Genesis 40) we read about Joseph interpreting the baker's dream. Is this sufficient evidence to prove that the Ancient Egyptians ate bread? What other evidence might there be that supports this? On a recent visit to Gainsborough Old Hall in Lincolnshire, the audio guide explained how bread was made in Medieval times and that a trencher was a piece of stale bread which was used as a plate. Stews and soups were put on the bread, and at the end of the meal the bread was eaten. This must have saved on the washing up! Should we just accept that this is historically accurate, or should the question be 'How can we be sure?'

As part of a topic about bread, children can be encouraged to question the reliability of different sources of evidence. Some commercial companies use the history of bread as a means of selling a traditional product. Some examples are:

- The Federation of Bakers and the Doves Farm website give a very comprehensive timeline for the history of bread from antiquity to the present day.
- Allison's Flour website has quite an interesting tribute to its Victorian founder, Thomas Allison, who championed a return to wholemeal bread in Victorian times because he believed it was important as part of a balanced diet. Children might then explore how this influenced Government policy for enriching white bread.
- The Hovis commercials on YouTube provide a short, lightweight glimpse into Hovis' past. In one case the three-minute video is the Victorian past and in a second, slightly longer, video the young lad is carrying his loaf of Hovis through time from the Victorian era, suffragettes, First and Second World Wars and arriving back home with the loaf to the present day.

What message are these companies giving, and which give reliable information about bread?

Why wholemeal?

Reading about Thomas Allinson's campaign for a return to eating wholemeal bread might lead children to question why wholemeal bread would improve the Victorians' diet. This question is best answered by researching for information and is an example of a *research investigation* (Turner et al., 2011). For older children, finding out about the different parts of a grain of wheat will develop their knowledge and understanding of its nutritional benefits. A good starting point is looking carefully at a grain of wheat. Diagrams of the inside of a wheat grain can be found in books or on the internet, for example on the Real Bread Campaign website. Older primary children might be interested to know that the fatter/plump end is known as the 'germ' which contains the wheat embryo, and today this is separated out to form the wheatgerm which can be found in health food shops. It is healthy because it contains the nutrients such as iron and certain vitamins which support the growth of the plant, so wheatgerm is often sprinkled onto cereal. This tiny germ section of the grain cannot be cut because of the oil content and only gets flattened, as is obvious when you look at a pack of wheat germ. Bran comes from the outer skins and can be made into bran flour or bran flakes. The endosperm when ground and sieved produces semolina and, when very finely ground, pure wheat flour.

From wheat to flour

Again, the supermarket and cupboards at home can provide a good starting point for an investigation about flour. A ten-minute look in our local supermarket gave me 23 different sorts of wheat flour, but where does the flour come from? In recent years concerns have been expressed about how little children know about the origins of the food they eat, and campaigns such as the Real Bread Campaign provide resources which help to address this.

Reverse sequencing is a good activity which can be used to explore children's knowledge of the origins of materials. Asking children to say where something comes from can be intrinsically interesting to the teacher, but more importantly it provides an insight into what children know before a topic is started. Start by asking them to draw a loaf of bread (Figure 6.2).

Figure 6.2 Where does bread come from? Reverse sequencing activity

Then ask them to draw what it was before it was a loaf of bread, then what it was before that, and what it was before that, going back as far as the child can, as outlined in the SPACE materials (Russell et al., 1991: 153). Figure 6.3 shows one child's ideas of where a loaf of bread comes from. They knew that bread was manufactured from wheat and that wheat is grown in a field, though a conversation with the child indicated that he did not know at what time of year it grew and did not link the harvest with wheat. He was also not sure about the changes involved throughout the process.

The leap from a sieve full of grain to a loaf takes huge imagination because technology today makes seeing how flour is made from wheat and then created into bread far less accessible than looking at how our Neolithic ancestors did it. So getting children to grind some wheat in the classroom is an important lesson in itself. Ideally pupils should see wheat

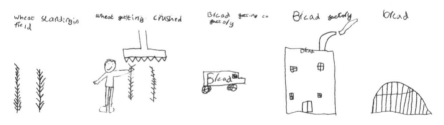

Figure 6.3 Reverse sequencing: one child's ideas about where bread comes from

Figure 6.4 Close observation of grains of wheat that have been ground

growing. There may be wheat growing nearer the school than you think, as some farm fields are very close to our urban schools and roads, but if necessary images of moving wheat fields can be found on the internet. It was only when a child closely observed and dissected an ear of wheat and then crushed the grains with a pestle and mortar that she recognized where flour came from. Figure 6.4 shows a child examining the flour they have made from grinding the grains taken from an ear of wheat. Notice the carefully labelled diagram showing different parts of the wheat, as it is in the fields.

The history of milling

Traditionally a rough sedimentary rock, such as millstone grit or a coarse sandstone, was used to make quernstones and later millstones to grind the grain into flour. Youtube (http://www.youtube.com/watch?v= RN9QFQXK1h8) provides a very short clip of two young French children using quernstones to grind grain into flour. The first couple of seconds does not require translation from French, but does give some idea of what hard work the original process would have involved. As the stones ground the grain, small pieces of the grit in the rock broke away. Flour with grit in would certainly wear teeth away more quickly. This may be a possible explanation for why the Neolithic teeth were so worn.

   In ancient civilizations wheat was ground by hand near the home or bakery; later the Romans and Ancient Greeks developed mechanical mills. They would have used animals or slaves to drive large wheels to grind the wheat – the use of horse power to turn the stones continued until the early Victorian era. By 1066, mills were common in most communities in England: the Domesday Book lists around 6,000 mills in England. The energy source, such as water or wind, used to work the machinery in the mill depended on its location, and children can be encouraged to investigate this. Finding evidence of mills in your locality can also be explored, either in class or as a class/home project. Historical traces of mills from the past can be found in many street names – Mill Street being the most commonly found, but also variations such as Corn Street, Bran Street and Grain Street. These are often the remains of Victorian terraced houses, built when the rural population was moving into the cities and required both increased grain and housing. Victorian mill owners built and rented out the houses in these streets, which would have been a huge improvement on the court housing their workers might otherwise have lived in. Even when the terraces have been replaced with newer housing, some of the street names remain. Also, it may be possible to arrange a visit to a historic mill which opens as part of a museum or heritage centre. An example is Stretton Water Mill near Chester, where two water wheels drive old wooden mill machinery which turn the millstones. The miller there shows how the machinery works, with its sieves and rollers, to transform the grain into flour. By the mid 1850s, flour milling was becoming much smoother and today nearly all wheat is milled by a roller mill process.

If children have ground some wheat by hand, comparisons can be made quite easily between this and flour bought from a supermarket. Children can generally see and feel how much rougher and coarser their rolling pin flour feels than the flour straight out of a packet. Using hand lenses or a digital microscope gives children an opportunity to look more closely at the difference in the particles between the flour they ground and the bought flour. The next step is to ask them to suggest how to get rid of some of the coarse pieces in their hand-ground flour, such as pieces of bran. The Romans, for example, sifted flour through linen for the really wealthy and were probably the first to start a milling industry to produce better and whiter flour for the less well off. The children could have a go at separating different-sized particles, using various sieves with smaller and smaller holes, eventually trying open weave fabric. This activity provides children with a genuine context for finding out about separating solids and for choosing the equipment suited to the task (Figure 6.5).

From flour to bread

Breadmaking provides a wonderful opportunity to explore changes to materials. We have already considered the changes from wheat to flour. Although these changes are not reversible, they are physical changes

Figure 6.5 Separating flour

because the chemistry of the wheat does not change, only the appearance. Baking bread provides an opportunity to look at chemical or irreversible change because when bread is made new substances are formed which are chemically different to the original ingredients.

When making bread children will be investigating by *observing change over time*, one of the five types of science enquiry that children need to cover as part of primary science (Turner et al., 2011). It is also is an activity which is suited to small-group work and can be supported by a teaching assistant or another adult in the classroom. The teaching assistant should be asked to direct the children's attention to the changes taking place as they make bread. They should discuss with children:

- whether the dough is a mixture or if it is something new that has been made
- how the dough has changed
- if they could get back to the material from the previous stage.

Keeping back a small amount of bread dough at each stage of the bread-making process helps children make comparisons (Figure 6.6).

In upper primary classes children could move on to develop *fair test investigations* to investigate some of the factors that affect how quickly bread dough rises: such as temperature or the type of flour or the amount of yeast. They can also investigate different types of raising agents.

Figure 6.6   How has the uncooked dough changed when it was baked?

Raising agents

Flour requires a raising agent to make the bread rise, which can be either yeast or a chemical raising agent. For soda bread this is usually sodium bicarbonate mixed with either yoghurt or sour milk. This combination causes a reaction which produces a gas, carbon dioxide, which becomes trapped as it bubbles through the dough. As the bread cooks these bubbles are set in the dough, producing a soft, sponge-like texture. Because new material is made, it is an irreversible or chemical change. Yeast produces the carbon dioxide needed to make bread rise through a process called fermentation. The yeast contains an enzyme which breaks down the carbohydrate in flour to sugar. The enzyme then breaks down the sugar to form carbon dioxide, which makes the dough rise, as well as alcohol.

Basic and easy bread recipes for bread rolls and soda bread can be found on The Grain Chain website so that children can make and taste the two different breads.

Making bread – historical evidence

Initially, the ground grain was made into a mixture called meal, which must have tasted dreadful. It was only when baking was discovered that it became possible to convert the flour into something much more enjoyable. It is thought that using yeast to make bread rise started in Ancient Egypt. The Cookit! website provides bread recipes for different periods of history and videos of cooking as it was done at different periods. One of these shows breadmaking in Tudor times. This provides an interesting insight into the lives of people in the past. However, to encourage the children to be historians, they should be asked to consider how reliable this evidence is. What other sources of evidence might support this?

The history of the baking profession can also be explored. It was only when researching for this chapter that I learned that some workers in Ancient Egypt were paid with loaves of bread. Also bakers were known to cheat their customers so bread assizes were introduced to regulate the weight of different loaves of bread.

The links between science and history

Throughout this chapter the science of breadmaking has been considered within a historical context. Similarities between science enquiry and historical enquiry have also been highlighted, particularly the idea that they use very similar enquiry skills such as raising questions, collecting evidence and checking its reliability. A group of science and history teachers in South Yorkshire who developed some cross-curricular science and history resources identified a number of similarities between the two subjects (Brodie and Thompson, 2009). We have used these to develop a tool to help teachers identify authentic links between subjects. Table 6.1 shows a completed grid using bread as the context for a cross-curricular unit of work.

A concern about cross-curricular work is that it is difficult to plan for progression in skills and knowledge. Progression in history skills have been teased out from the National Curriculum level descriptors for history by Rowley and Cooper (2009: 13) – see Table 6.2.

Table 6.1 Planning tool for making cross-curricular links explicit: completed grid for bread

TOPIC: BREAD

How does the subject provide:	Science	Other subject: history
An interesting starting point or context for learning?	Trip to museum and seeing Neolithic teeth Trip to supermarket bakery to see different kinds of bread and bread being made.	
Opportunities to practise skills? Use this list to help you plan the specific links between science and your chosen subject: • Asking questions • Collecting evidence • Manipulating evidence • Classifying • Observations • Similarities and differences • Looking critically at the evidence • Drawing conclusions • Validity of evidence (NB: Only choose those skills which are relevant to the unit of work you are planning for)	**Asking questions:** e.g. Why are the breads different? What does wheat look like? How can we make flour? **Collecting evidence** Close observation of: • different types of bread • an ear of wheat • types of flour (use digital microscope to aid observation) • types of bread Look for **similarities and differences** between the breads **Sorting** a range of breads **Science investigations:** Observing change over time as bread is made Fair test investigation – How does temperature affect time taken for dough to rise? How does the type of flour used affect the time taken for bread to rise?	**Asking questions:** Why were the teeth damaged by eating bread? **Collecting evidence:** e.g. Pictures of farming, milling and baking from Ancient Egyptian or Ancient Greek paintings Recipes for bread from Tudor/Victorian times Look at **similarities and differences** between bread recipes, e.g. Tudor bread and present day bread **Historical investigations:** Where was our local mill? Did both rich and poor in Tudor times eat the same types of bread? When did bakers first use tins to bake bread in?

How does the subject provide:	Science	Other subject: history
	Draw conclusions Use evidence from flour investigation to suggest why white bread became popular	**Draw conclusions** Use evidence about how wheat was milled in olden days to explain why teeth were damaged
Opportunities to develop the children's subject knowledge?	Where does bread come from? What are the changes that happen when making bread? Reversible or irreversible changes at each stage of breadmaking Bread in a healthy diet	How has the type of bread eaten changed throughout history? What developments in farming, milling or baking have made these changes possible? Bread and diet? Why bread flour was fortified to improve diets

Opportunities to communicate their ideas?

English – Writing for different audiences – propaganda leaflet to encourage eating fortified bread

ICT – Time-lapse photos for stages of proving bread

Digital microscope to see textures of different types of bread

Table 6.2 Progression in history skills

	Questions	Investigation	Opinions
Level 1	Find answers to	Use sources of information to answer simple questions	
Level 2	Observe or handle sources of information to answer questions about the past on the basis of simple observation	Recognize that their own lives are different from those of the past	Beginning to recognize why people in the past acted as they did
Level 3	To answer questions about the past	Use sources of information in ways that go beyond simple observation	Beginning to give a few reasons for, and results of, main events and changes
Level 4	Produce structured work	Begin to select and combine information from different sources	Give some reasons for, and the results of, main events and changes

Task 6.1

The topic of bread, as described in this chapter, can provide learning opportunities for children across the primary age phase to practise enquiry skills in both history and science. Use Rowley and Cooper's progression chart (Table 6.2) in conjunction with the planning tool for making cross-curricular links (Table 6.1) to help you consider what expectations you would have for a Year 3 class.

If you have access to *It's Not Fair – Or Is It?* (Turner et al., 2011), you may wish to see how this links to progression in science skills.

References

Brodie, E. and Thompson, M. (2009) Double crossed: cross-curricular teaching of science and history. *School Science Review*, 90(332): 47–52.

Furedi, F. (2009) *Wasted: Why Education Isn't Educating*. London: Continuum.

Hughes, P. (2008) *Principles of Primary Education*. London: Routledge.

Rowley, R. and Cooper, H. (2009) *Cross-curricular Approaches to Teaching and Learning*. London: Sage.

Russell, T., Longden, K. and McGuigan, L (1991) *Materials*. Liverpool: Liverpool University Press. Available at http://www.nationalstemcentre .org.uk/elibrary/file/15730/SPACE%20Materials.pdf [accessed 29 May 2012].

Short, K., Schroeder, J., Laird, J., Kauffman, G., Ferguson, M. and Crawford, K. (1996) *Learning Together Through Inquiry: From Columbus to Integrated Curriculum*. Maine: Stenhouse.

Turner, J., Keogh, B., Naylor, S. and Lawrence, L. (2011) *It's Not Fair – Or Is It? A Guide to Developing Children's Ideas Through Primary Science Enquiry*. Sandbach: Millgate House and Hatfield: ASE.

Websites:

The Federation of Bakers: http://www.bakersfederation.org.uk/the-bread-industry/history-of-bread.html [accessed 28 May 2012].

Doves Farm: http://www.dovesfarm.co.uk/about/the-history-of-bread/ – a commercial farm website, but includes recipes and a history of bread from Neolithic times through to the Chorleywood Bread Process [accessed 28 May 2012].

The Real Bread Campaign: http://www.sustainweb.org/realbread/schools/ – part of a general UK campaign aimed at 'fighting for better bread in Britain and finding ways to make bread better for us, better for our communities and better for the planet'. Special section for teachers [accessed 28 May 2012].

The Grain Chain: http://www.grainchain.com – supported by the Federation of Bakers, the Grain Chain is UK-based and provides what the writers describe as 'tailor made teaching materials, worksheets, videos, quizzes, recipes and activities about farming, milling and baking'. There are separate sections for Key Stages 1 and 2 [accessed 28 May 2012].

Allison Flour: http://www.allinsonbread.com/ [accessed 28 May 2012].

http://www.newgrange.com – overview and DVD of the wonder and mystery of Newgrange Neolithic site, Stone Age passage tomb [accessed 28 May 2012].

The Cookit! website: http://cookit.e2bn.org/historycookbook/ – includes the History Cookbook, which contains podcasts, recipes, galleries, background information and activities relating to cooking from prehistoric times to the post-war period; it provides a rich cross-curricular resource with a multitude of applications [accessed 28 May 2012].

7 Religious education enhancing science

Mark Hamill

Task 7.1 Pre-reading task

Before beginning this chapter, take a few minutes to reflect on your own thoughts concerning the relationship between science and religion. If you have strong feelings on this issue, consider what may have caused these. How do your personal feelings affect how you teach science and religious education? Are you wary about children asking you difficult questions in this area to which you may give answers that are inaccurate or may be insensitive to a particular group?

The purpose of this chapter is to help you to navigate the relationship between science and religion and to understand that your teaching of science can be enhanced by bringing into play some of the concepts and ideas that feature in religious education.

The relationship(s) between science and religion

Research by Taber et al. (2011) has revealed that a significant proportion of Key Stage 3 students believe that an insurmountable conflict exists between science and religion. Though I am unaware of any similar research having been conducted with primary pupils, I, from my own experience, and colleagues and student teachers working in primary schools report similar responses when the topic of the relationship between science and religion is touched upon. 'Science disproves God', a Year 6 pupil confidently informed me once at the outset of a religious education (RE) lesson, thus prompting me to completely abandon the learning objectives related to the five Ks in Sikhism that I had just shared with the rest of the class, and explore instead the pupils' conception of 'truth'.

A widespread acceptance of the 'science versus religion' conflict thesis by British citizens of all ages would come as no surprise given the media (over)exposure of celebrity atheist and agnostic scientists such as Richard Dawkins, who are famously antagonistic towards any religious truth claims and provocatively describe religious belief as 'a virus of the mind'.

Yet, according to Cantor, ideas of conflict 'are not adequate as general claims about how science and religion have been interrelated in history ... Much historical research has invalidated the conflict thesis' (1991: 290). In fact, any talk of a relationship between science and religion is anathema to Brooke; rather 'it is what different individuals and communities have made of it in a plethora of different contexts' (1991: 321).

Barbour (2002), however, has attempted to categorize the different relationships that have existed between science and religion down the centuries. He notes that the conflict thesis is a product of the modern age, having first arisen in the nineteenth century. (Galileo's problems with the Vatican were apparently more personal and political than ideological. Copernicus had dedicated the book in which he had set out the revolutionary theory of a heliocentric universe to the Pope in 1543, 60 years prior to Galileo setting his eye to a telescope.)

In what is perceived to be in direct contrast to the conflict thesis, Barbour also identifies the 'integration' thesis as another way in which the relationship between science and religion has functioned throughout history. Even the most evangelical atheist cannot deny that Western science, as we understand it today, has its origins in a theistic world view. Most, if not all, of the giants upon whose shoulders Hawking, Dawkins, Cox et al. now stand, were theists. Roger Bacon, who is credited as one of the fathers of the scientific method, was a thirteenth-century monk. Isaac Newton spent more time on theology than he did on science. Gregor Mendel, who demonstrated 'inheritance' through his study of pea plants in the nineteenth century, was an Augustine friar. In common with their Muslim counterparts, these Christian scientists believed that the study of nature (the works of God) and the study of Holy Scripture (the word of God) were complementary activities that, to borrow a phrase from Johannes Kepler, allowed the scholar 'to think God's thoughts after Him'. Many contemporary scientists of all faiths continue this tradition of 'integration'. Former Director of the Human Genome Project, Francis Collins, is but one example. 'As a scientist who is also a believer, I find exploring nature also to be a way of getting a glimpse of God's mind' (quoted in Sweeney, 2007).

High-profile disputes between individual scientists and members of the Church hierarchy in the nineteenth century, especially over the matter of Origins, helped to further the process of severing science from its ecclesiastical patronage and heritage. Barbour claims that this separation of science and theology has not always been conceptualized as a cause of conflict, and proposes 'independence' and 'dialogue' as his final two categories.

Gould (1999) has popularized the 'independence' thesis through his invention of the NOMA (non-overlapping magesteria) principle. Science and religion inhabit separate worlds – the physical and the spiritual respectively. They should not try to claim authority beyond their own borders.

According to the 'dialogue' thesis, the borders are still preserved but it is possible for the two parties to have words across them. If the only agreement possible in the conflict thesis is that the other party is inherently 'wrong', in the dialogue thesis, both parties can maintain the belief that they are inherently 'right'.

Task 7.2

Which of the four ways of thinking about the science–religion debate outlined in this section is closest to your personal view? Why might this be?

Imagine that you are the subject leader for science in a faith school. Which of these positions should you adopt? How might this be different if you led the subject in a non-denominational school?

Science and religious education in the primary school

The relationships that have existed and continue to exist between science and religion may provide some insight into the relationship that ought to exist between the curriculum subjects of science and religious education in the primary school. In a faith setting, it is appropriate for all subjects to point ultimately towards the Divine. In a science lesson in a Christian faith school, a teacher might encourage her pupils to report the findings of their experiments honestly by an appeal to the Biblical injunction on 'bearing false witness'. In a lesson on caring for animals, the same teacher might invoke the Christian concept of 'stewardship' – the Christian belief that humans are mandated by God to take care of His creation. In faith settings, science and other curriculum subjects, including religious education, should be taught as part of the religious education that the pupils are receiving. Therefore, for faith settings, the integration thesis is most relevant. Consequently, a diagram representing the relationship between religious knowledge and scientific knowledge in a faith school might show the latter as residing wholly within the former.

In non-denominational settings, all subjects can be taught without the need to invoke God or holy texts, although there is nothing currently in British law preventing individual teachers of faith in such schools from doing so. As the conflict thesis is both historically unjustified and highly inappropriate for the primary school, the majority of teachers in non-denominational settings are left with the 'independence' or 'dialogue' theses to choose from. Due to the title of this chapter and the thrust of this whole book, readers should not be surprised that the dialogue thesis is the one that is advocated for non-denominational schools. Diagrammatically, you might have represented this relationship as two separate spheres from each of which arrows emanate into the other. This also might be how, in previous chapters of this volume, you represented the relationship between scientific knowledge and historical knowledge or geographical knowledge. As is argued elsewhere in this volume, allowing a dialogue between science and all curriculum subjects is essential for good science teaching in the primary school. For, as Thacker (quoted in Cooling, 2010) points out, 'Science can only be properly understood or applied when it is put in its social, historical, philosophical, ethical and religious context.'

But before I proceed to give examples of how a dialogue between the subjects of science and religious education can help to enhance teaching of the former, it has to be acknowledged that dialogue is, of course, a two-way process. As a consequence of allowing science some input into my RE lessons, my teaching in this area has also been greatly enhanced. For example, in helping primary pupils to comprehend the central Hindu concept of *brahman* – the impersonal and invisible life force that constitutes the only reality in the universe – I have often turned to pupils' knowledge of the theory of gravity. Like *brahman*, gravity is an invisible force that causes objects to act in certain ways. I have then asked pupils to personify (a concept that they have learned in English) gravity. Their subsequent drawings usually turn out to show people of an age when gravity is most exacting on the human form. According to Hindu teaching, *brahman* creates, sustains and destroys life. These three essential aspects are also represented in the persons of the deities, Brahma, Shiva and Vishnu. Pupils then study images of these three deities, looking for clues as to which deity personifies which aspect of the *brahman*.

My use of a scientific concept to help pupils to understand the religious concept of *brahman* has a historical precedent. In the Vedas, one of Hinduism's many holy texts, there is an account of what must be the oldest primary science lesson ever recorded. A teacher presents his pupil with two glasses of water. Unknown to the pupil, the teacher has dissolved a lump of salt in one of the glasses. The student is asked to note any differences between the water in each glass, using only his eyes. No differences are apparent. The student is then invited to drink from each glass. The difference is now obvious. Though it was invisible, the dissolved salt permeated all the water in the glass. This, the teacher explains, is how *brahman* is, invisible yet fully present.

What is true for science and religious education is true for all the other subjects that form the primary curriculum. Each can enhance the other in a variety of ways, for example concepts in mathematics can enhance learning in music, history can help to inform the context in which poems studied in English were written, and cross-country running in physical education (PE) lessons can benefit from a knowledge of geography!

Religious education: learning about and learning from

It is now common practice in religious education, whatever the setting, that pupils learn both *about* and *from* religious beliefs and practices. For example, in a sequence of lessons on the Ten Commandments, pupils will not only learn about the Commandments and the context in which they were given, but must also have the opportunity to reflect on the significance of these rules, and rules in general, in their own lives. This requirement 'to learn from' is unique to religious education and gives it the potential to be the most engaging and demanding subject in the primary curriculum. It also makes the subject a powerhouse in contributing to pupils' social, moral, spiritual and cultural development which, since 1944, in schools in England, has been a requirement on all curriculum subjects, including science.

Task 7.3

How do your views of religion or your religious beliefs influence the way you teach certain science topics?

These statements were made by children in a church school:
   'You get day and night because God has special gloves and he picks up the sun and moves it out of the way.'
   'God turns a handle to make the Earth spin round.'

How would you respond to these children? How is your response influenced by your own personal beliefs? How would you respond if you taught in a non-denominational school?

Discuss your views with a colleague.

Commentary

Having reflected upon what pupils might learn *from* your science lessons, and having discussed this with your colleague, you might come to the conclusion that they learn very little in this regard. Science, you might contend, concerns itself with facts. What could possibly be the personal significance of knowing that 'pure' water freezes at 0° Celsius and boils at 100° Celsius?' A number of objections could be raised to this view.

Firstly, pupils cannot help learning something *from* your lessons. If you teach in a way to suggest that science has no personal meaning or significance, they will learn this and, as a consequence, will give up the study of science at the earliest possible point. (I write from personal experience as someone who opted out of school science at 13.) Secondly, by 'teaching the facts and nothing but the facts', you are abdicating your role as a science educator for, as Cooling points out, 'learning to make judgements about the meaning and the significance of what we learn is actually what education is all about' (2010: 13). If you fail to do this in your science lessons, your children might as well learn their science from BBC Bitesize.

RE-enhanced science in practice: resisting reductionism

The National Curriculum for science at Key Stages 1 and 2 requires pupils to learn about life processes and living things. In this area of study, pupils should be taught among other things that:

- animals, including humans, move, feed, grow, use their senses and reproduce
- humans and other animals need food and water to stay alive
- the life processes common to humans and other animals include nutrition, movement, growth and reproduction.

There is a grave danger in this area of undermining the uniqueness of the human species. While the above statements are empirically true, the needs and accomplishments of humans represent much more than is conveyed here. As well as considering what we have in common with other forms of life, which is undoubtedly important and a particular focus of many religious traditions, pupils also need to consider that which makes us unique, including our urge to ask the question 'Why?' – an urge that gave rise to both science and religion.

A simple sorting exercise could be developed for Key Stage 1 pupils. At Key Stage 2, a teacher might devise a sorting exercise that includes the higher primates and/or a computer. Key Stage 2 pupils might also attempt to provide an account of the profound differences between humans and the higher primates given that we share an estimated 98 per cent of the same genetic material.

Extension work from this exercise, looking at the difference between humans and robots, might involve Key Stage 2 pupils designing their own version of the Turing Test to discover if a participant is able to distinguish whether they are communicating with a human or a computer. A hand-held Twenty Questions electronic game could be used in this experiment. There are also many online versions. The Disney film 'Wall-E' is a very useful resource for exploring these issues further. A question that could be asked after watching the film is: 'How have science and technology changed the humans in the film?'

Primary teachers need to be alive to the risk of reductionism in other sections of the National Curriculum for science. Arthur Jones, a former re-search scientist and an educational consultant to faith schools around the world, has written extensively on how most science teaching in schools occurs within a world view that promotes economic utility as the highest good. In a highly insightful piece on the subject of calcium, Jones (1998) demonstrates how most science textbooks focus primarily on the indus-trial uses of this element and ignore its many other properties in its natural position, such as its aesthetic and recreational qualities in the form of lime-stone pavement. Though Jones's piece was written for a secondary school audience, I believe that his point has direct relevance for primary teachers.

Task 7.4

Think about the last time you taught the science topic of materials and their properties. Did you encourage children just to focus on the properties of a material related to their uses, or did you guide them to think about the aesthetic nature of materials and provide the opportunity for them to give an emotional response? Following Jones's example, consider how you might include awe and wonder in your teaching of a topic about wood.

Science and religious education: investigating the mysterious

Humans ask 'Why' in the face of mystery. Mystery is a concept like God Herself that lies at the heart of religious education. The concept of mystery, however, is an affront to many scientists, who justifiably believe it has been used in the past to prop up illegitimate hierarchies and mask intellectual laziness. They, like Dorothy in the Wizard of Oz, would tear back the curtain to reveal the unremarkable truth. They believe that, given time, science will be able to answer all questions and banish all mysteries. A world devoid of the mysterious, in which all things can be known, is one that strangely lacks appeal and stifles the human spirit. For inspiring science to occur in primary schools, a sense of mystery has to be retained and some questions have to remain unanswered.

In this regard, I would recommend the work of Rupert Sheldrake (1995, 2012), an unorthodox (some would say heretical) scientist and author who, in his writing, attacks what he terms 'scientific dogmatism', accusing his peers of deluding themselves with 'the recurrent fantasy of omniscience'. For Sheldrake, the world is far more mysterious than conventional science believes it to be. To investigate the mystery beyond the scope of conventional science, Sheldrake has devised experiments into human and canine perception, one of which poses the question, 'Can humans detect being watched by an unseen viewer?'

Inspired by Sheldrake's work, I challenged my class of Year 5 pupils to answer this question. They devised their own experiments that involved firstly the members of the class and then Reception pupils, adult staff and parent volunteers. The pupils were rigorous in the planning and the running of the tests that they devised and in recording their results. Taking account of chance as best as they could, my pupils, like Sheldrake, recorded positive results to the research question. Of course, the finding of my pupils did not definitively prove that humans can perceive being watched by an unseen viewer, and in fact other studies going as far back as the late nineteenth century (see Titchener, 1898) have debunked the theory.

However, apparently undaunted by the realization that their results were anomalous, my pupils embarked independently upon a study into another mystery – the mystery of yawning. 'What causes us to yawn?' 'Is seeing another person yawn sufficient stimulus or do you have to hear them yawn as well?' 'Is merely reading about yawning enough to make you yawn?' (You may feel an irresistible urge to yawn at this point, although this may be due to my style of writing!) 'Are younger people more responsive than older people?' 'What about other animals?' These were only some of the research questions that the pupils generated.

Yawning and 'extra-sensory' perception may not feature in the National Curriculum for primary science, but they are examples of 'the mysterious' that helped inspire some of the best and most authentic science lessons that I delivered as a classroom teacher. Science in schools must, therefore, not declare a crusade against the mysterious but instead allow it to inspire. Such work, of course, takes one beyond the content of the National

Curriculum that provides the context in which 'scientific enquiry' is to be pursued. It is no coincidence that the subtitle of Sheldrake's most recent book is 'Freeing the Spirit of Enquiry' (2012). At time of writing, the National Curriculum has mandatory status in maintained schools. Therefore, teachers wishing to 'free the spirit of scientific enquiry' are advised to do so during a school's Science Week or in an after-school science club.

Edward Jenner and (not) perpetuating the mythical conflict thesis

To overcome the myth of the conflict between science and religion, teachers might want to share with pupils the life stories of famous scientists of faith. At the time of writing Edward Jenner is the only scientist mentioned by name in the National Curriculum for science at primary level. A teacher wishing to humanize a study of vaccination might include the story of Jenner's discovery and some biographical material. The second website produced by a Google search on Edward Jenner is that of the BBC, a trusted source of information for teachers in the UK and throughout the world. In a well written and succinct passage on Jenner's life and work, the following assertion is made by the anonymous author.

'Jenner was widely ridiculed. Critics, especially the clergy, claimed it was repulsive and ungodly to inoculate someone with material from a diseased animal' (BBC, date unknown).

While it may be true that some members of the clergy (together with non-ordained men and women of science) opposed Jenner's work, many others in holy orders supported him. The Reverend Dr John Clinch, a lifelong friend of Jenner, a fellow scientist and a missionary in Newfoundland, began vaccinating his local populace only six months after Jenner had vaccinated his first subjects. It is thought that the vaccine used by Clinch had been brought to Newfoundland by Jenner's nephew, also an ordained Christian medical missionary. Despite the alleged ridicule of the clergy, Jenner himself continued to attend weekly worship at his local Anglican Church, St Mary's Berkeley, until his death in 1823. So, no doubt, Jenner's own vicar was not included among his ecclesiastical critics. Though it is difficult to establish definitively, it is not unreasonable to surmise that Jenner's determination to eradicate smallpox derived from his Christian faith as much as his spirit of scientific enquiry. In recognition of the enormous contribution Jenner made to the Church's mission of alleviating human suffering, a statue of Jenner now stands in the nave of Gloucester Cathedral.

Teachers should exercise caution and carry out wider research before exposing pupils to sources that perpetuate the mythical 'conflict' between science and religion.

Conclusion: lame science, blind religion

Albert Einstein wrote, in a letter to philosopher Eric Gutkind, that 'Without religion, science is lame; without science, religion is blind'. The first half of this famous quote provides the perfect summation of the argument advanced in this chapter. Without allowing elements of religious education to enter your science lessons, the science that you teach will be inert and will fail to contribute to your pupils' social, moral, spiritual and cultural development. On the other hand, as suggested in the second part of the quote, science can enhance religious education lessons by fully 'opening the eyes' of older pupils in particular to the contexts in which religious beliefs and practices develop.

References

Barbour, I.G. (2002) *Religion and Science: Historical and Contemporary Issues.* Norwich: SCM Press.

BBC (date unknown) Edward Jenner: 1749–1823. Available at http://www.bbc.co.uk/history/historic_figures/jenner_edward.shtml [accessed 29 May 2012].

Brooke, J.H. (1991) *Science and Religion: Some Historical Perspectives.* Cambridge: Cambridge University Press.

Cantor, G. (1991) *Michael Faraday: Sandemanian and Scientist.* Basingstoke: Macmillan.

Cooling, T. (2010) *Doing God in Education.* London: Theos.

Gould, S.J. (1999) *Rocks of Ages: Science and Religion in the Fullness of Life.* Michigan: Ballantine Books.

Jones, A. (1998) *Science in Faith: A Christian Perspective on Teaching Science.* Worcester: Christian Schools' Trust.

Sheldrake, R. (1995) *Seven Experiments that could Change the World: A Do-It-Yourself Guide to Revolutionary Science.* New York: Riverhead Books.

Sheldrake, R. (2012) *The Science Delusion: Freeing the Spirit of Enquiry.* London: Coronet.

Sweeney, J. (2007) *Speaking of Spirituality.* Available online at http://www.explorefaith.org/speaking_collins.html [accessed 18 Mar 2012].

Taber, K.S., Billingsley, B., Riga, F. and Newdick, H. (2011) To what extent do pupils perceive science to be inconsistent with religious faith? An exploratory survey of 13–14-year-old English pupils. *Science Education International*, 22(2): 99–118.

Titchener, E.B. (1898) The feeling of being stared at. *Science* 8: 895–7.

8   Art enhancing science

Sharon Harris and Alison Hermon

This chapter aims to explore the natural links between the visual arts and science, with an emphasis on enquiry and exploration generated through investigating a variety of materials and processes. It will draw upon the creative potential in making connections between the two subjects, while also seeking to retain their unique identities.

Why teach art and science together?

Art may not be the first subject the majority of teachers would think of pairing with science. However, centuries ago in the time of Galileo, Leonardo da Vinci and Robert Hooke, there were no such barriers to linking the two. The polarization of the arts and sciences has been a comparatively recent one, highlighted in C.P. Snow's *The Two Cultures* (Snow, 1959), but one which is now once again firmly in the spotlight in terms of the connectivity between the subjects. There already exist a number of high-profile collaborative projects between art and science, including the Wellcome Foundation's 'Sciart' programme, Science, Art and Writing (SAW) in schools, the Chem@rt initiative, The Leonardo Effect and Creative Partnerships.

Children do not compartmentalize learning – adults do it for them, either through interpreting the National Curriculum in prescriptive and restrictive ways in school, or through the polarized representation of the subjects in the media. The separation of the arts and sciences begins early, but this does not need to be the case. This separation seems surprising when we begin to recognize inherent relationships and see that there are many more commonalities than differences – including the practical, investigative, visual and creative nature shared by both. For instance, in both art and science, teachers use processes such as working from close observation as children engage first hand with a range of living and non-living things. This helps teachers in both subjects to build on children's innate curiosity and stimulate their imagination, using all their senses to explore and discover the amazing secrets of objects. Eisner (2002: 5) states that the arts encourage us 'to look hard, to savour the qualities that we try under normal conditions to treat so efficiently that we hardly notice they are there'. A number of strategies for making science engaging and creative have been identified by Oliver (2006: 26–9) and include 'making the ordinary fascinating', 'sharing a sense of wonder' and 'seeing differently', which will be revisited later in the chapter as part of examples of good classroom practice.

The world around us is a constant source of inspiration, awe and wonder, especially to children who may be experiencing a material, object or process for the first time. Is there a teacher who is not still surprised by the delight of a child in working out for themselves how to make a bulb in a circuit light up for the very first time, or in the iridescence of colours in bubbles they have just created? Giving children time and opportunities for exploration can encourage them to think and act creatively, as seeing differently might also entail attitudes of open-mindedness, expecting the unexpected, or finding more than one solution to a problem – perhaps the antithesis of the traditional view of science as being essentially factual, logical and predictable?

Why teach art in a cross-curricular manner?

Perhaps it is not so difficult to see why art might be considered to be a subject that lends itself to cross-curricular work when it appears to be naturally linked to a range of subjects and areas of learning. This is particularly the case in the Early Years, when children begin to make art. Duffy has recognized that 'children use their representations to explore, to solve problems, to think about and create new meanings. Different forms of representation enable them to address problems in various ways and gain new insights' (Duffy, 2006: 11). This example demonstrates the value of art as a useful opening to learning experiences in other subjects, and recognizes how children develop as a whole and how aspects of development are interlinked.

> The arts are increasingly seen as a way of joining up the curriculum and making it meaningful to young people. Through the arts children express their feelings, thoughts and responses. The arts have the potential to stimulate open-ended activity which encourages discovery, exploration, experimentation and invention.
>
> (Duffy, 2006: xvi)

In the primary phase, we know that art, like other subjects in the curriculum, has its own skills, processes and knowledge base. But it is unhelpful to disregard the interchange of processes and ideas between similar learning experiences in different areas, knowing that subject boundaries are artificial constructions. Making links between subjects can help deepen and extend knowledge and understanding in many ways. For instance, investigating the work of land artists may enhance learning in science concerning the properties of the materials chosen, of habitats and environments and the organisms that live in them, as well as developing understanding of ecological issues.

From this perspective, we can accept that working in cross-curricular ways will help us to recognize the importance of learning *through* art in addition to learning *in* art. In other words, we value learning opportunities for extrinsic as well as intrinsic reasons, for example when creativity and processes are emphasized for their significance for children's learning in holistic ways above other things. Depending on the learning situation, this may include valuing art's contribution to children's well-being and/or social interaction. Meager (2006) has recognized the exciting and empowering potential of cross-curricular learning with a strong art focus when undertaking collaborative work. He identifies the importance of teachers providing a skeletal framework, 'helping children create their own meanings as they work both individually and within a group, communicating ideas' (2006: 15). Working on a class project, children may share and cooperate, valuing the contributions of others, and learn to listen and compromise before making final decisions. This is also true when children carry out scientific enquiries, almost always collaboratively.

Despite subject divisions, the National Curriculum (DfEE/QCA, 1999) recognizes cross-curricular opportunities in all subjects including art, identifying how learning might extend to other much broader areas such as thinking skills. Eisner (2002: 85) believes that art is a powerful means of connecting with the world, using transferable ways of thinking to heighten our perception. This includes taking an approach we might use when making or appreciating art, including the use of our senses and our feelings, sensations and emotions, and to 'map' this approach onto the world around us, as it 'provides frames for reading the world', seeing and noticing things we might otherwise forget.

Overall, there is a great deal of potential for developing a range of transferable skills when working with art in cross-curricular contexts. Either independently or collaboratively, children are encouraged to learn to think and act in innovative ways, to address challenge constructively, and to show initiative in finding imaginative solutions to problems.

What makes art special and different from science?

The field of art has a key role to play in influencing and enriching our lives, using a unique, primarily visual language to communicate ideas, thoughts and feelings. According to Eisner:

> The prime value of the arts in education lies in the unique contributions it makes to the individual's experience and understanding of the world. The visual arts deal with an aspect of human consciousness that no other field touches on: the aesthetic contemplation of visual form.
>
> (Eisner, 1972: 9)

Visual language

We need to recognize that art is primarily a visual mode and as such art can be thought of as a visual 'language'. Children need to know how to use it, developing knowledge of the different visual elements. For this reason, processes linked with observation and explorations are key features of art education. However, if both art and science use the visual world and the senses, particularly visual perception, what is special about art, and how is it different from science particularly when science draws on the world as a resource? According to Herne et al. (2009: 28), in art 'we are not just dealing with perception: we are trying to teach visual aesthetic perception'. From this perspective, drawing in science is a means of recording knowledge through the process of observation, whereas in art it is hoped that children will also develop artistic vision while representing reality, and communicate this in an informed and imaginative way. Drawing not only helps young artists to record what they have seen, it also leads them to see further (Berger, 1960).

However, a word of warning here might be appropriate. One of the pitfalls to avoid is the simplistic view that any type of observational drawing is 'art' in itself. Student teachers, for example, have thought that they had made links with art simply by getting children to draw round each other's bodies as part of a topic on 'ourselves'. Certainly, this could lead to interesting art-based learning, but not when used merely to 'service' the science. However, as a stimulus, Arnold suggests that 'Pictures and the processes that go into producing them seem to provide a vehicle by which artists and scientists can talk to each other' (Arnold, 2000: 80).

Eisner (1972: 9) identifies art as a unique form of 'human consciousness' which is characterized by particular qualities and capabilities. This involves knowledge of visual language as discussed above, specific art materials and experiences, as well as people involved in creating art. Children are encouraged to develop knowledge of artists, craftspeople and designers to gain inspiration for their own work and broaden their awareness of ideas. From past to present, works of art, craft and design have offered powerful revelations about local cultures, the cultures of others and other historical contexts. They offer insight into the human and social condition as well as making valuable and responsible contributions to social change and development. What makes art unique can be defined by these areas.

At the same time, it is important to recognize that developing knowledge of visual language can also foster children's intellectual development, help them understand feelings and explore values. For instance, children learn that art involves making judgements about work, helping them develop higher order thinking skills. Keeping an open mind is key to this process, involving taking thoughts and action in new directions. Strong links can be made with science as both subjects recognize problem-solving, reflection and openness to change (Chessin and Zander, 2006). At the same time, both offer scope for children to become more sensitive and responsive to their environment and to think critically about these areas. Recent research in cognitive development strongly argues the case for the place of the arts in terms of connecting person and experience, recognizing the role of 'emotional thought' in heightening learning. Indeed, the developing field of neuroscience has identified a range of factors contributing to overall brain development.

Individuality

It would also appear that developing and communicating individual identity in the development of artistic vision is of key importance, which Eisner (1972: 9) recognizes as 'the individual's experience and understanding of the world'. Thus individuality is intrinsic to the artistic process, fostering a sense of one's own identity and the identity of others. For children, making art is seen as a vehicle for personal growth through shaping, making sense of their surroundings and expressing personal vision. Subjective opinion and artistic interpretation are both valued. Children are encouraged to be creative and imaginative through experimenting with ideas, materials and visual elements to help generate individual responses. Such experiences require openness to change, to expect the unexpected, take informed risks, be flexible in thinking and develop autonomy. This promotes distinctive ways of understanding the self, realizing individual abilities and feeling empowered.

These features which contribute to developing personal vision in art are also characteristics of learning in science. In both art and science, the teacher can promote choice and use a range of sources to recognize individual strengths. Personal selection is a key feature in motivating children to learn, to maintain their interest and to follow ideas along individual pathways. Sharing these with others develops their awareness of the potential to communicate certain values, qualities and meanings from the perspective of different individuals. If this is the case, we need to question what is special about art and what makes it different from science in relation to these areas. According to Kemp:

> A work of art always remains open for interpretation, drawing the spectator into the shape of the artist's visualisation, but without being able to exert fixed control over the feelings it induces. There is always room for the beholder's share. Scientists may wish to engage the reader or spectator in a wonderful journey of imaginative visualisation, but in the final analysis they wish to communicate an interpretation that embodies testable content in an unambiguous way.
>
> (Kemp, 2005: 309)

Using the aesthetic dimension of visual art may help in drawing children into the science, helping to create a desire to explore further and to communicate their ideas in unusual and creative ways.

It is important to recognize that both art and science can benefit from collaboration in raising the status of both subjects as being of equal importance in the minds of teachers and learners (Robson et al., 2008).

Hidden worlds revealed – sharing a sense of awe and wonder

Microscopes have long been a source of vizualizing the invisible world. From the intricate drawings of Robert Hooke's insects in *Micrographia* (1665) to the images of Ernst Haeckel (1904) portraying the amazing complexity of tiny sea creatures named radiolarians, magnification has enabled us to engage with the natural world on a level of detail previously hidden.

Observation with the aid of lenses, microscopes and visualizers can enable really close encounters with ordinary objects, which then reveal their amazing secrets in detail. Such instruments allow us to see beyond the obvious, to wonder and to question. Ede (2005) poses the view that scientific images in themselves are not art, no matter how colourful or beautiful. There must be some engagement with an interpretative dimension which allows an aesthetic response from both the artist and the viewer, a 'unique take on the world, which they [the viewers] are at liberty to reinterpret' (Ede, 2005: 188). On the other hand, Kemp (2004: 506) wonders whether we should worry about whether scientific images constitute art or not and instead, 'say that any implicit competition between artists and scientists as makers of wonderful images is rather beside the point'.

There are many ongoing creative collaborations between artists and scientists, making use of new technologies such as the scanning electron microscope (SEM). The work of Rob Kesseler in this field with his interpretations of plant material, including pollen grains, seeds and fruits, has provided inspiration for projects using digital microscopes, now widely available in schools. Indeed, Kesseler acknowledges the impact of his father bringing home a light microscope bought in a junk shop when he was 11 years old, which 'revealed a mesmerizing parallel universe to explore', with far-reaching consequences in terms of his future (Kesseler, 2010: 128).

Visual imagery, especially of the unusual, provides a vehicle for capturing the imagination and for developing curiosity. Awe and wonder become the starting points of investigation and exploration. Virtually any material may be explored, both natural and man-made. A project on fruits, seeds and vegetables, for example, lends itself to children cutting different sections and observing patterns, colours and shapes. They can then hypothesize about their nature and function.

Images can be captured at different magnifications, saved and manipulated through software applications. The images themselves can become stimuli for further observation and interpretation, this time from a more aesthetic viewpoint. For instance, children can record from observation of digital imagery or primary sources in wax resist to explore the patterns and colours of specimens using wax crayon and watercolour. They can then develop this further, investigating other materials and techniques such as the resist effects of batik, creating lines and patterns in hot wax using tjanting tools and brushes to simulate particular effects. Applying colour can be achieved by using brush-on dyes or drawing inks to realize different colour mixtures and combinations fairly immediately.

Hidden worlds are again revealed as children are introduced to the 1951 Festival of Britain Pattern Group scientists and designers (Jackson, 2008) collaborating on a range of vibrant designs inspired by atomic structures using x-ray crystallography. Some of the intricate designs in lace and fabric reflect qualities achieved with a tjanting tool or brush dipped in molten wax. Such approaches lend themselves to imaginative and individual ways of working, providing children with opportunities to make informed choices and take risks as wax resist can be unpredictable. This will support them in making unlikely connections as well as challenge their ideas – key characteristics of creativity (Figure 8.1).

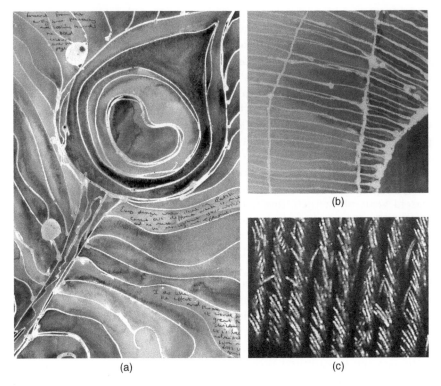

Figure 8.1 The evolution of images produced from a peacock feather

At the other end of the scale, images of the universe from the Hubble Telescope can be used as a stimulus for investigating the macrocosmos. Images from Hubble are created from multiple data streams from different cameras, originally in black and white. They are then coloured using digital technologies (similar to Kesseler's SEM images) to enhance specific features or to show detail that the unaided human eye might miss.

Pattern and colour close up – making the ordinary fascinating

Plants provide an endless source of material for artists and scientists to work with and from which to derive inspiration. Scientifically, plants are the key to all life through their ability to photosynthesize, producing sugars and oxygen. They are the basis of the vast majority of food chains and the source of a vast range of products and materials. Yet children

Figure 8.2 Leaves in the style of Andy Goldsworthy

often need encouragement to engage with plants, despite their knowledge being limited in comparison with animals. However, there are many aspects which lend themselves to closer examination through the eyes of an artist/scientist and can provide a 'way in' to motivating interest and excitement. We shall focus on pattern and colour here.

Children can begin by collecting a colour palette of leaves, especially in autumn, and transforming them into crowns or ephemeral art in the style of Andy Goldsworthy, a widely known artist working in the environment (Figure 8.2). In doing so, they can be encouraged to carefully observe features such as colour, leaf shape, patterns in venation, texture and size. In art they will learn the importance of natural materials for inspiring art in the environment, exploring specific visual elements like colour, pattern and composition, and recognize how such works depend on different characteristics of the environment including geology and climate as well as the effects of time and seasons. They will undertake research of Andy Goldsworthy to recognize how and why he works in these ways. They will explore the possibilities of creating their own compositions, considering specific processes such as layering and arranging, recognizing the importance of individual interpretation and the potential for creating pieces in previously unexplored sites. In science, these observations can form the basis of classifying and identifying enquiries, sorting leaves according to a variety of characteristics, using data-handling skills to present sets in the form of Venn and Carroll diagrams or in making branching keys. Key Stage 2 children can research why leaves change colour in autumn.

In art in both Key Stages children can create crayon or pencil rubbings of leaves and then use a variety of printing methods, which become more complex depending on the Key Stage. For instance, working from observation initially, children explore a variety of leaf patterns in line drawing. They are encouraged to develop this as a design for a block print to create

Figure 8.3 Leaf prints made by Year 2 children

a repeat pattern, being shown examples of leaf and plant motifs in printed textiles. Through observation of samples they understand how they can create a variety of pattern with one unit by repeating it across the page, including 'half drop' and rotating it around an axis. They create a block print from either press print (compressed polystyrene) or string or glue blocks (Figure 8.3). Alongside this, they print with natural objects such as leaves and other natural forms like fruits and vegetables directly onto paper or fabric. They can create a final composition using a range of approaches and collaborating with a partner. They consider particular colours when thinking about which printing inks they will use.

These experiences can then be used to help children make creative connections between ideas, processes and materials, with future work

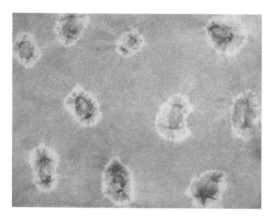

Figure 8.4 Using plant dyes

continuing with other resist techniques like shibori (tie and dye). From a scientific perspective, individuals can investigate the properties of natural dyes, threads and fabrics to achieve particular effects, for example the unusual and unexpected patterns produced by rusting as they embed nails and other metal objects into shibori and dye experiments (Figure 8.4). Such opportunities encourage children to make unlikely connections and to challenge their own views.

On the surface, the dry brown papery skins of onions would seem only destined for the compost bin and yet they may be transformed by a scientific process in the production of natural dyes. While this process provides a context for tie and dye in art, it allows exploration of changing materials in the science curriculum. Obviously, before beginning the work, an appropriate risk assessment needs to have been carried out. The onion skins are boiled in water in an old saucepan for 15–20 minutes, but if no cooker is available, near boiling water from a kettle will work well enough if the skins are left to soak and the liquid stirred periodically. The result is a pale brown liquid similar to weak tea in colour. However, the colour is transformed into bright yellow with the addition of a type of chemical salt called alum (aluminium potassium sulphate). This acts as a mordant, meaning that it not only changes the colour but makes the dye colourfast. Children will be fascinated by the use of stale urine (boys' was apparently considered the best!) as a mordant in the past. Salt (sodium chloride) is commonly used when using commercial dyes and may be used as a substitute for alum, although different mordants produce different colour effects.

This comparatively simple process can be a trigger for questions which can then form the basis of fair test enquiries with a host of variables to investigate, including time, temperature, type of fabric, type and quantity of mordant and when it is added. (Check with the Association for Science Education (ASE) (2011) or CLEAPSS (http://www.cleapss.org.uk) which are safe to use.) Factors such as colour take-up in different fabrics or colour fastness with or without a mordant can be investigated. The enquiry can be extended through the use of different plant materials (will red onion skins make a red dye?). Beetroot, berries, tea and red cabbage work well. Other things affect the changes in the way the dye adheres to the materials. For example, adding vinegar or bicarbonate of soda will change red cabbage dye into red or green according to its acidity, since it is a natural indicator of acidity.

Natural landscapes – seeing differently and looking beyond

Using the natural landscape can involve selecting environmental artists like Lynne Hull and Chris Drury (Drury and Syrad, 2004) as starting points for learning with a Key Stage 2 class. Through investigation and creation of environmental sculpture this can increase children's transferable knowledge and understanding of habitats, considering shelter, protection and food. Initially, children collect objects from nature, take photographs and make sketches while exploring the aesthetic qualities of environmental pieces by artists. Investigating the work of ecological artist Lynne Hull and undertaking a visit to a site such as Chris Drury's Heart of Reeds in Lewes, East Sussex, helps children recognize how living land sculptures can be made to support local wildlife.

Back in school, pupils can investigate the process of weaving in the natural and made world, observing how nests are created by particular birds, insects and small animals before working on simple looms with a range of threads and materials (Figure 8.5). Through these experiences children will begin to recognize the ecological dimension of artists' works, the interrelationship between humans and the creatures and how their actions impact on the environment and culture.

Another important area is to recognize the potential of working collaboratively with other partners and to consider how such an approach can offer unexpected creative opportunities for all involved. Working in partnership with a venue like the Kew Botanic Gardens at Wakehurst Place, West Sussex, site of the Millennium Seed Bank (MSB), where there is an identified link between art and science through Kew's Big Draw annual programme of events, can provide a starting point for work in art and science. At Wakehurst Place there is a focus on using the gardens and the MSB

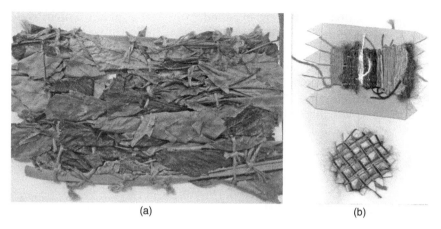

(a)   (b)

Figure 8.5 Weaving inspired by the natural world

to inspire art activities while informing the public about the scientific work being carried out. For instance, in 2009 the autumn half-term theme was 'Colouring by numbers' including 'Netting seeds', an activity celebrating the MSB's achievement of collecting 10 per cent of the world's flowering plant seeds. Part of the programme offered visitors, including children, the opportunity to make close observational drawings of a range of different seed types, both common and unusual, with microscopes available to help them look closely. They were then able to produce monoprints from these drawings which were finally sewn onto netting banners on the windows of the MSB, with every tenth print being orange to highlight the 10 per cent achievement (Harris et al., 2011).

An evaluation from a student teacher recognized how this activity was successful on many levels:

> It encouraged both children and adults to engage with artefacts they may have not seen before. They were introduced to different ways of looking at objects. This encouraged children's naturally curious nature and ultimately they were able to create a piece of work from their experience. The Big Draw encourages visitors to galleries, museums and rural spaces to connect with artefacts, ideas and concepts in new and exciting ways. The MSB certainly achieved this.
>
> (Student teacher evaluation, 2009)

These experiences clearly have close links with the aims of *Learning Outside the Classroom Manifesto* in recognizing the importance of making provision for quality learning experiences in real contexts which 'can lead to a deeper understanding of the concepts that span traditional subject boundaries and which are frequently difficult to teach effectively using classroom methods alone' (DfES, 2006: 3). You may not have such a resource in your immediate locality, but similar opportunities could be identified and activities adapted in a local park or even within the school grounds, encouraging children to engage with the environment on their doorsteps.

Light and shadow – creative collaborations

Exploring a shadow puppet theme offers potential for a range of learning opportunities in art and design. In relation to learning in science, initially pupils can experiment with shadows and light sources behind a screen made of a simple wooden frame with cotton stretched over the top. It would be helpful to investigate the materials of shadow puppets. For instance, traditional puppets are made from the skins of animals punctured with tiny holes and decorated with paint. Others are made from a combination of hide and carved and painted wood. In order to explore these sources, pupils would need to understand the contexts of making, relating to different cultures like India and Indonesia. Pupils can look at film footage of extravagant shadow puppet plays which are accompanied by the sounds of the Gamelan orchestra. In terms of a project for creating in art, links to science can be made through the choice of subject matter to inspire a shadow puppet play such as minibeasts or the natural world. Working from starting points like the picture books of Eric Carle (*The Very Busy Spider*, *The Very Hungry Caterpillar* and *The Bad-Tempered Ladybird*), young children can look at the shapes, patterns and colours of insects from different sources including textbooks and weblinks on insects and butterflies. The investigating and making and knowledge and understanding programmes of study will be addressed very thoroughly through this process, including exploring visual elements: art, craft and design from a range of different contexts from the past and different techniques for creating.

There are a number of processes involved in making different types of shadow puppets. These include making black shadow puppets cut from card and then simply punctured using a hole punch. Colour can be introduced by tissue paper or cellophane taped to the back. Puppets can be animated by making moving parts with simple mechanisms using split pins and sticks. Coloured puppets can be made by colouring white card with water-based agents like paint and pen and then oiling to make them more translucent. Another option which is particularly immediate for younger children is bubble wrap and tissue collaged together or coloured paper doilies to make beautiful butterfly shapes.

This links very closely to investigating the quality of shadows using a range of opaque, translucent and even transparent objects. How can coloured shadows be made? How can the size of the shadow be changed, and what happens to its clarity? What is the effect of using a range of different light sources? Compare using a point light source such as a bulb in a simple series circuit with a more diffuse light source such as a reading or table lamp. If you still have an overhead projector (OHP), this makes an excellent source for creating coloured backgrounds on the flat screen as well as providing a bright light to illuminate the puppets.

A shadow puppet theatre is one of the best contexts for cross-curricular work, not just in art and science, but also in design and technology (including making moving parts) and not least in encouraging speaking and listening. In our experience it is the ultimate motivational collaborative project for children to work in groups exploring, creating and developing their own ideas.

References

Arnold, K. (2000) Between explanation and inspiration: images in science, in S. Ede (ed.) *Strange and Charmed*. London: Coclouste Gulbenkian Foundation: 68–83.

Association for Science Education (ASE) (2011) *Be Safe!* Fourth edition. Hatfield: ASE.

Berger, J. (1960) *Permanent Red*. London: Writers and Readers.

Chessin, D. and Zander, M.J. (2006) The nature of science and art. *Science Scope*, 29(8): 42–6.

DfEE/QCA (1999) *The National Curriculum Handbook for Primary Teachers in England*. London: Department for Education and Employment/ Qualifications and Curriculum Authority.

DfES (2006) *Learning Outside the Classroom Manifesto*. Nottingham: DfES. Available at https://www.education.gov.uk/publications/ standard/publicationdetail/page1/DFES-04232-2006 [accessed 5 Apr 2012].

Drury, C. and Syrad, K. (2004) *Chris Drury: Silent Spaces*. London: Thames and Hudson.

Duffy, B. (2006) *Supporting Creativity and Imagination in the Early Years*. Buckingham: Open University Press.

Ede, S. (2005) *Art and Science*. London: I.B. Tauris.

Eisner, E. (1972) *Educating Artistic Vision*. New York: Collier-Macmillan.

Eisner, E. (2002) *The Arts and the Creation of Mind*. New Haven, CT: Yale University Press.

Haeckel, E. (1904) *Art Forms in Nature*. Revised edition, 1974. New York: Dover Publications.

Harris, S., Hermon, A. and Allan, S. (2011) Drawn together. *Primary Science*, 120: 32–4.

Herne, S., Cox, S. and Watts, R. (2009) *Readings in Primary Art Education*. Bristol: Intellect Books.

Jackson, L. (2008) *From Atoms to Patterns*. London: Wellcome Trust.

Kemp, M. (2004) A fluid definition of art. *Nature*, 429: 506.

Kemp, M. (2005) From science in art to the art of science. *Nature*, 434: 308–9.

Kesseler, R. (2010) *Up Close*. London: Papadakis.

Meager, N. (2006) *Creativity and Culture: Arts Projects for Primary Schools*. NSEAD: Collins Educational.

Oliver, A. (2006) *Creative Teaching: Science in the Early Years and Primary Classroom*. London: David Fulton.

Snow, C.P. (1959) *The Two Cultures*. Cambridge: Cambridge University Press.

Robson, D., Hickey, I. and Flanagan, M. (2008) The Leonardo effect: art and science working together. *START Magazine for Primary and Preschool Teachers of Art, Craft and Design*, 29: 26–8.

Useful websites:

Chem@rt: http://www.chemlabs.bris.ac.uk/outreach/primary/WhatIs-Chemart.html [accessed 14 Apr 2012].

CLEAPSS: http://www.cleapss.org.uk/ [accessed 29 May 2012].

Creative Partnerships: http://www.creative-partnerships.com/about/ [accessed 4 Apr 2012].

Chris Drury: http://chrisdrury.co.uk/ [accessed 13 Apr 2012].

Hubble: http://hubblesite.org/ [accessed 14 Apr 2012].

Lynne Hull: http://eco-art.org/ [accessed 13 Apr 2012].

Rob Kesseler: http://www.robkesseler.co.uk/ [accessed 13 Apr 2012].

The Leonardo Effect: http://www.leonardoeffect.com/ [accessed 14 Apr 2012].

Science, Art and Writing: http://www.sawtrust.org/ [accessed 14 Apr 2012].

The Wellcome Foundation SciArt: http://www.wellcome.ac.uk/Funding/Public-engagement/Funded-projects/Awards-made/All-awards-made/WTX035067.htm [accessed 14 Apr 2012].

9 Design and technology enhancing science

Liz Lawrence

Science and design and technology (D&T) have been linked, either formally in the curriculum or by making connections in and between lessons, since before the advent of the National Curriculum but the assumptions that underlie this relationship have changed over the years. In his article, 'The relationship between science and technology in the primary curriculum – alternative perspectives', Davies (1997) draws heavily on Gardner's 1994 framework for categorization of views on this relationship. This proposes five positions:

1 Science and technology as indistinguishable.
2 The demarcationist view – science and technology as independent activities with different purposes and methods.
3 Technology as applied science, with technological capability made possible by scientific knowledge. Technology is dependent on science, with technologists taking abstract scientific ideas and making them useful.
4 The materialist view, where technology precedes science and knowledge of concepts arises from designing, making and interacting with functional artefacts. In this view, science is dependent on technology for both the equipment which enables new discoveries and the ideas which lead to models and theories.
5 The interactionist view, which sees the subjects as equal and complementary. Each subject draws on the other as necessary to achieve its own subject-specific goal.

Before the development of the National Curriculum for England and Wales, science and D&T were often seen as components of a combined area of learning – science and technology – characterized by problem-solving activities which allowed children to learn skills and discover concepts concurrently. This approach persisted into early National Curriculum discussions but all versions of the National Curriculum which have been legislated into use have identified them as separate subjects with their own programmes of study and assessment criteria. Although changes to the curriculum in 1995 (DfEE, 1995), when Sir Ron Dearing was charged with the removal of subject content overlap, reinforced a demarcationist approach, many teachers continued to recognize the links in their classroom practice.

In its 1998 technology policy (ASE, 1998), the Association for Science Education (ASE) expressed the belief that:

> science and the two main aspects of technology, information technology and designing and making (often known as 'design & technology') are inextricably interwoven. For this reason it is important to foster both the natural relationship between science and design & technology and develop the distinctive characteristics of their component parts.

The new primary curriculum (QCDA, 2010) built on this view in drawing the two subjects together in a 'scientific and technological understanding' area of learning. Although criticized by some as risking the loss of separate identities, the subjects still remained distinct with links in content and methodology emphasized. The statement from this area of learning, 'Science supports the development of technology and advances in technology lead to new scientific discoveries' (QCDA, 2010: 60), exemplifies an interactionist view of the subjects where each at times services the needs of the other without becoming subsumed. However, the use of technology as shorthand for design and technology caused great consternation as it implied an applied science view, which did not fully recognize the nature of D&T.

Loose use of terminology, plus misunderstandings about D&T, has confused many recent curriculum development debates. The single word 'technology' can be understood to refer to information and communication technology (ICT) or to describe the process of making or crafting machinery and artefacts. Neglect of the fundamental place of designing in the subject, coupled with confusion about the nature of the design process, is responsible for dubious decision-making at both policy and classroom levels.

Although an interactionist view is implicit in many of the examples in this chapter, the relationship between science and D&T in the classroom varies between units of work and either subject may provide the starting point and drive the learning. Motivations for linking vary from the pragmatic need to make the most of limited teaching time to the recognition that such links can provide engaging contexts in which to develop and extend understanding and capabilities. The most effective of these interactions are based on a clear understanding of both subjects. This allows teachers to make explicit to the learners the distinct objectives for each subject as well as identifying how they work together in a particular project or unit of work. It also ensures that work in both subjects is pitched at an appropriate level.

In a primary project poster, 'Vehicles – Let's go to the showground', The Design and Technology Association adapts the standard unit of work on wheeled vehicles for 6- to 7-year-olds to include testing which materials would improve the grip of tyres on a steep bridge. All the D&T elements are retained, with an additional opportunity to use investigative skills and to begin to learn about friction, relating it to a developing knowledge of the properties of materials. In this case the D&T provides both a context and a need for the related science activities which inform the design process.

A teacher with good subject knowledge and a clear rationale for linking will also recognize occasions when the subjects are best taught separately and attempts to force links will be detrimental to learning in one or both subjects. The following examples illustrate projects which do not allow for sufficient objectives, at the right level, from both subjects to be met.

- Designing and making a textile product such as slippers fulfils many D&T objectives at a suitable level for 10- to 11-year-olds but any associated science is likely to be revision of material properties thoroughly explored lower down the school, with limited scope for extending understanding or for new learning relevant to the key concepts taught at that stage.
- Film canister rockets launched by a simple chemical reaction provide many opportunities for science enquiries, but the addition of cardboard cones and fins to the canister, although providing additional variables to investigate, is unlikely to develop into a valid D&T activity.

Such activities are still useful for stand-alone teaching of science or D&T and may link to other subjects, but for a project to develop effective science and D&T links for learning it must meet age-appropriate objectives from both subjects and provide a context in which the learning will be better than if they were taught discretely.

The same cannot be said for a further subset of projects, often arising from another subject, which meet neither D&T nor science objectives, although they may have some value within the original subject context.

These include such historically inspired model-making activities as building a Viking longboat – which, due to limitations of historical understanding and available materials, is unlikely to involve any meaningful designing or to allow for serious investigation of floating and sinking or properties of historically relevant materials.

An article in the ASE journal, *Primary Science* (Lawrence and Lunt, 2011), describes work undertaken jointly by ASE and The Design and Technology Association on linking the two subjects, one outcome of which was several 'Science and D&T: Making Effective Links for Learning' workshops at conferences. The Design and Technology Association brought to this work a checklist, 'Essentials for Design and Technology', which they had developed as a way to address misconceptions about the nature of the subject and ensure that projects included all the elements needed for good D&T learning.

Essentials for design and technology

- Do the children have a clear idea of the **user(s)** they are designing and making products for so they can aim to address their needs, wants, interests or preferences?
- Do the children know the **purpose** of the products they are designing and making? Can they evaluate the tasks they do in use?
- Are the children making informed **design decisions**, for example what the product will do, how it will do it and the materials, components and techniques they will use to make it?
- Do the children's products work/**function** rather than being purely aesthetic?
- Are the children encouraged to be **innovative**, developing a range of design ideas and products?
- Are the children designing and making **authentic** products which are meaningful to them rather than models or replicas?

Further information and guidance relating to these essentials is available on the Design and Technology Association website.

To mirror the above criteria and inform the joint working, ASE produced a list of science essentials.

Essentials for science

- Does the activity have a clear **purpose** and **context** understood by the children?

- Are the children obtaining **evidence** to answer their questions by gathering data directly by observation or measurement, or by using secondary sources?
- Are they **authentic questions** (ones which pupils do not know the answer to and have been involved in generating)?
- Are the children involved in **planning decisions**?
- Is evidence being used and challenged to draw **conclusions** and develop **explanations**?
- Is there **new scientific learning** which challenges and extends children's **existing science ideas**? Are **skills** being developed?
- Are children **communicating** their observations and findings in an effective, scientific way?

These combine key features of the enquiry process with a focus on the acquisition of scientific knowledge and practical skills, recognizing that links between the two subjects work at different levels.

One way of considering these links is at the level of transferable skills. If we look from the viewpoint of the product design and production process there are clear matches between the four elements of *discover, define, develop* and *deliver* and the skills which are intrinsic to science enquiry.

- *Discovery*, where the need is identified and the original idea for a product is generated, involves observation, hypothesizing and questioning.
- In the *define* phase, where the product idea takes shape, there is further collecting of evidence to test the initial hypothesis about the potential user and purpose and to clarify what is both required and possible. There will also be communication of information, visually and concisely, using labelled and annotated drawings and diagrams.
- During *development*, research into materials, components and techniques and the testing of prototypes uses skills of collecting, presenting and interpreting data and communicating results.
- The *deliver* phase, where the final product is produced and marketed, draws upon the scientific outcomes from earlier phases but will also include the collection of data to evaluate the performance of the product and compare it with competitors.

Science and D&T also develop skills of systematic planning and evaluating as well as the more generic skills and attitudes needed for collaborative working, problem-solving and creative thinking.

Task 9.1

Think of a topic you have taught or might teach which you think will make effective links between science and D&T. In your planning, when will the children be given the opportunity to:

- ask and find answers to their own questions?
- include all the essentials for D&T and science?
- use different types of science enquiry? (A useful resource which gives a comprehensive guide to different types of scientific enquiry is *It's Not Fair – Or Is It?* (Turner et al., 2011).
- use D&T which involves product investigations, focused practical tasks and designing and making products?

What science knowledge do the children need to inform their designs?

The industrial process above can be related to the designing and making stage of a D&T unit of work, but children also need to be involved in investigating and evaluating existing products and in focused practical tasks (FPTs) which teach skills and knowledge needed for the later designing and making. Product evaluation may involve considering the properties of the materials used, describing how (and how well) a mechanism works or comparing products using scientific tests – which coolbag is the most effective? Which type of biscuit is best for dunking in tea? Many focused practical tasks will be specifically technological, such as using a hole punch and split pins to make simple levers or practising sewing a seam, but scientific investigations into the properties of materials or testing how well different glues will join specific materials could be described as FPTs with a science emphasis.

From this it could be argued that all D&T projects provide the scope for children to develop skills which are also used in science and can therefore be effectively linked. The examples given earlier of non-productive contexts may provide superficial opportunities for science, but for links to be most effective there should be a clear science enquiry process, the acquisition of scientific knowledge or a deepening of understanding through application of knowledge in a challenging new context. Well integrated science and D&T projects will meet the criteria set out by Barnes (2011: 10): 'When the skills, knowledge and attitudes of a number of different disciplines are applied to a single experience, problem, question, theme or idea, we are working in a cross-curricular way.'

Figure 9.1   Children use a light sensor to test possible materials for Ricky's sunglasses

In addition to the consideration of skills, many D&T projects require scientific knowledge for their successful completion. This may be application of existing knowledge, in which case the benefit to science is in consolidating or deepening, or it may be in stimulating enquiry (practical or research) which results in pupils acquiring new knowledge.

Children making puppets or simple garments will need to consider which materials to use. This could involve revisiting a number of familiar properties such as softness, flexibility, strength or stretchiness in relation to the product and user. For younger children this will be age-appropriate and, unlike in the earlier slippers example, is likely to embed learning which was not previously secure. By changing the design brief to include further requirements such as a garment which is windproof or high visibility (as in the 'Teddy's Safety Jacket' project on the Design and Technology Association's primary website), additional properties can be highlighted.

A project to design and make sunglasses for Ricky the puppet, from the Ricky Explores Antarctica website, provides the stimulus for investigating a new property, linked to a different area of science – how well different materials transmit light – and results in new learning about transparent, translucent and opaque materials and the effects of using different coloured filters (Figure 9.1).

Research and guidance on science enquiry has explored the relationship between the methodology of science and D&T. In the AKSIS[1] publication,

---

[1] ASE-King's Science Investigation in Schools Project.

Developing Understanding in Scientific Enquiry (Goldsworthy et al., 2000), one of the types of scientific enquiry identified by the authors is making things or developing systems, also referred to as a technology enquiry and defined as designing, testing and adapting an artefact or system. Examples provided include a pressure pad switch for a burglar alarm and a vivarium for woodlice. In their more recent book, *It's Not Fair – Or Is It?* Turner et al. (2011) rethink the AKSIS classification of enquiries, describing five different types: Observing over time, Identifying and classifying, Pattern seeking, Research, and Fair testing. Instead of allocating enquiries which result in children making something to a separate category, they recognize that enquiries of different types may lead to a range of different outcomes: 'Children solve a problem, answer a question, develop an explanation, make and evaluate an artefact or system, provide evidence to justify why the outcome is appropriate or raise more questions to investigate' (Turner et al., 2011: 12). Designing and making products is seen as one way for children to demonstrate and apply the learning resulting from their enquiries but also as a stimulus for those enquiries, depending on how the unit of work is structured.

As for other contexts, the default option for science enquiry linked to D&T tends to be the fair test. Fair testing, which develops both scientific and generic transferable skills, is well suited to informing the decision-making processes involved in designing and making. It may be used during the design process when choosing materials for their specific properties, as in the earlier example of making sunglasses, and testing prototypes. Or it may be used as part of the final product evaluation, where structures may be tested for strength, shopping bags for how effectively the handles distribute the pressure, or torches for how well they enable us to find objects in the dark. But, as shown by the examples below, some of the questions arising from or informing the D&T project will initiate other types of enquiry.

One example from the AKSIS project, the designing and making of a vivarium, could be introduced as a problem-solving activity which initiates scientific activity – How can we keep woodlice in our classroom so we can observe them more closely? – or it may be the culmination of a study of minibeasts, where children demonstrate through designing, making and testing their vivarium that they have an understanding of the needs of woodlice and the habitat in which they are found. Depending on the starting point, the scientific activities will either be generated by the needs of the D&T project or the project will be an application and consolidation of scientific learning. In both cases the children can undertake a range of scientific activities to inform the design process, for example:

- Identifying and classifying enquiry – can they distinguish woodlice from other minibeasts they may encounter?

- Finding out about the habitat where woodlice live – pattern-seeking to determine where and in what conditions woodlice live.
- Finding out what woodlice eat by observation over time and/or research.

There are fewer opportunities for D&T objectives to be met, but decisions will need to be made about the container (size, shape, material) and the contents of the vivarium. The project would rank highly for authenticity, user, purpose and function but much lower for innovation and design decisions and would have little scope for working with tools and techniques.

Another example, the burglar alarm, provides a different balance between science and D&T. Children will explore electric circuits, including a range of switches and output devices, providing simple explanations and communicating in diagrams, using standard symbols. They will also classify electrical conductors and insulators. They will use this knowledge to design and make a suitable switch and include it in an alarm circuit with visual and/or audible output. The focus can be broadened from a burglar alarm to consider other types of alarm or warning system, giving children opportunities to test their alarms in real situations or on purpose-built models. Once again the product may be an application of what has been learned in a science topic (an outcome) or a stimulus for the scientific learning, but will have involved children in one or more of identifying and classifying, observing over time, pattern seeking, fair testing or research rather than being a distinctly technological type of enquiry.

As well as awareness of the science and D&T approaches and skills which an effectively linked project needs to include, teachers need to consider where the project fits into the curriculum as a whole and what will provide the starting point. Bianchi and Thompson (2011: 53) state that:

> The range of approaches [to cross-curricular science planning] ... includes:
>
> - making a link
> - a topic or topic web – not very integrated
> - an integrated topic
> - a personalized topic – pupil-led approach based on enquiry

Making a link is the simplest of these: knowledge and skills from one subject are drawn on in lessons of another subject. Children exploring mechanisms use their knowledge from an earlier science unit of work when describing how a friction drive works; children testing which of their vehicles travels the furthest are reminded about the need to control variables.

The personalized approach is the most difficult to include unless it forms the basis of whole-school planning approaches. For productive science and D&T links to develop, the teacher needs to consider the initial stimuli with great care and be very aware of progression in the two subjects, ensuring that outcomes are appropriate to the subject and the stage of development of the children.

Topics are a more usual vehicle for cross-curricular teaching and these come in different forms. Some are only nominally cross-curricular, with subjects linked by little more than a common title but, at the other end of the continuum, a well integrated topic approach can build powerful connections between the learning in different subjects. Working on classroom projects and continuing professional development with colleagues Bobbie Gargrave and Jim Scott, a version of a planning web has been developed which identifies how subjects within the topic or theme are linked. We have found that it works best for three subjects; more can be included, as in the example, but the links to additional subjects may be incomplete. We suggest that a larger theme involving more subjects could be broken down into two or three shorter sequential subtopics, each closely linking a smaller number of subjects.

In this example (Figure 9.2), developed for teaching to 5- to 7-year-olds, the story book *Penguin Small* (Inkpen, 1992) is used as the overall theme for

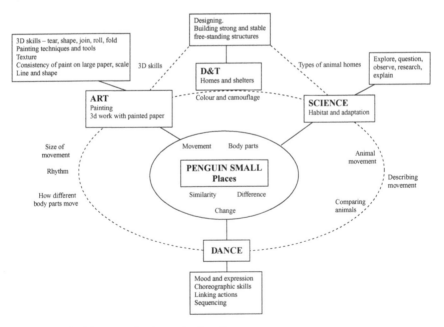

Figure 9.2 Planning for *Penguin Small*

several weeks' work, with the focus for this specific topic narrowed down to features of the different places he visits and the creatures who live there. The main subjects involved are science, art and dance. The central circle identifies the elements that all the subjects have in common – these rather than the topic title form the basis of the linking, moving the focus from something general to more specific common elements of the learning. Links shared by only two of the subjects are written between them on the dotted circle and subject-specific elements are in boxes beyond the circle. For this topic D&T is beyond the circle – it has links to the science and art but does not link with dance or include the elements shared by all the other subjects.

Dance

Children explore the animals individually, relating their movements to descriptions in the story – 'The bears were in a terrible mood'; characters are described as hovering, diving, whizzing and gliding – and to the different environments. They work in groups to create fantasy animals such as Hooter crabs and the Neverwozanoceros by making linked shapes that can move.

Art

Children use rhythmic large and small body movements (fingers, wrists, moving whole arm and upper body while standing) to create large communal paintings. When dry, these are used as a sculptural material to make different places which can be populated by imaginary creatures, made using similar techniques, or used as scenery for the dance.

Science

Using the real and imaginary animals in the book as a starting point, children ask and investigate questions such as:

- How do real animals move?
- What body parts do they need for different movements?
- How does this link with where they live – adaptation?
- What colours are the animals? How does this help them?
- How might this imaginary animal move? What makes you think that?
- What might an animal that lives here look like?
- Are there other birds which can't fly? How do they move?

Figure 9.3 Paper sculptures of imaginary creatures

D&T

Children design and make camouflaged shelters for different real or imaginary creatures and habitats. These may include working with sheet materials, using techniques from the art objectives, and with natural materials (Figure 9.3).

Somewhere between making a link and topics involving multiple subjects sit projects whose primary purpose is to link only science and D&T, integrating the two and building on the specific features of those subjects which make them naturally complementary. In the article 'Making Effective Links for Learning' (Lawrence and Lunt, 2011), models of linking were identified which lead to a range of starting points for such work.

Some projects develop from a science unit of work with the D&T outcome being an application or extension of the newly acquired scientific knowledge. Following investigations into temperature and thermal insulation, children can design a range of products from insulated lunch bags to earmuffs for a cold day. This could be presented as an open-ended opportunity to demonstrate what they have learned, by designing and making a product of their choice or a more specific problem-solving challenge leading to a range of products with the same function.

In other cases the design brief becomes the stimulus for the science activities. If the D&T draws on only one area of science, as in the earlier example of designing and making an alarm system, the shape of the unit may be very similar to the example above with children learning specific content from one science unit in order to inform their decision-making in D&T. However, this type of project also lends itself to including more than one area of science, breaking down some of the barriers which segregate science content in many schemes of work. In the Primary Update activity 'Ricky's Shelter', children design and make a shelter or tent for Ricky the puppet to use on his Antarctic expedition (available as one of the free downloads at http://www.primaryupd8.org). This starting point generates questions as varied as:

- How cold does it get in Antarctica?
- Does the colour of the tent make a difference?
- Is waterproof the same as snowproof?
- Why does Antarctica not get dark in summer?
- How can I make my tent dark enough so I can sleep? (Figure 9.4)
- Why do people sleep better in the dark? Is it the same for other animals?
- Which shape of tent is best for windy conditions?
- How strong is the wind in Antarctica?
- How much weight can a person carry or pull?
- Which materials will melt if you have a camping stove in your tent?

Figure 9.4 How can I make my tent dark enough so I can sleep?

The resulting enquiries, of various types, cover properties of materials, light, forces, Earth, Sun and Moon and ourselves. Projects of this type can provide strong motivation as the learning has a clear purpose for the children and is generated by their own questions, but does not fit into many science schemes of work as easily as less wide-ranging activities. In some cases the science will extend beyond the requirements of the D&T as the original enquiries generate further questions, for example further investigations of strength and endurance following from the initial consideration of how light the tent would need to be.

Making a shelter for a specific location and conditions could be a stand-alone unit of work, but the Ricky Explores Antarctica project also provides an example of another planning model, where a broad context or topic generates a number of smaller integrated projects which may each cover different areas of science and D&T. Although links between them may be limited to the overall context, unlike the topic web approach each individual project has strong cross-curricular links within it. The ideas on the Ricky website, in addition to tents and sunglasses, include gloves, a pulley system for crevasse rescues and a safety helmet (Figure 9.5). If this expedition was used as the basis for an extended unit of work, children may suggest other useful products as well.

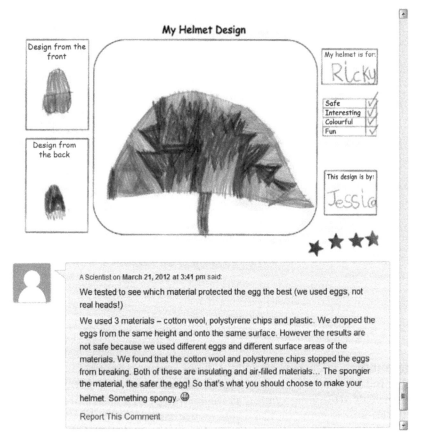

Figure 9.5 Child's design for Ricky's helmet

The range of possible products and contexts demonstrate that science and D&T links can take many forms and be achieved in different ways, through content, skills and process. There are also occasions when link-ing can be forced or detrimental. The best links exemplify Bianchi and Thompson's (2011: 53) principle that 'Learning experiences are more relevant when children's questions and interests play a part in driving the curriculum design, and subjects and skills combine to build a series of interconnected experiences.' The overriding concern within this is to ensure that what is taught and learned is good D&T, involving all the elements of the designing and making process at a suitable level, and good science, with a range of enquiry types leading to the development of science knowledge and its application in real contexts. The key question is always: will the learning in *both* subjects be improved by teaching them together?

Task 9.2

If you were given the following topics as part of your long-term planning, which would you teach as a stand-alone D&T activity or which would you teach as a stand-alone science activity, and why? Which topics make opportunities for effectively linking science and D&T?

- Designing and making musical instruments
- Designing and making photo frames
- Mixing and separating materials
- Microorganisms

If you choose the topic yoghurt instead of microorganisms, could you make a more effective link between science and D&T?

References

Association for Science Education (ASE) (1998) *Technology: Design and Technology* (policy statement). Hatfield: ASE.

Barnes, J. (2011) *Cross-Curricular Learning 3–14*. Second edition. London: Sage.

Bianchi, L. and Thompson, P. (2011) Science within cross-curricular approaches, in W. Harlen (ed.) *ASE Guide to Primary Science Education*. Hatfield: ASE: 53–60.

Davies, D. (1997) The relationship between science and technology in the primary curriculum – alternative perspectives. *Journal of Design and Technology Education*, 2(2): 101–11. Available at http://ojs.lboro.ac.uk/ojs/index.php/JDTE/article/viewFile/462/439 [accessed 14 Apr 2012].

DfEE (1995) *Science in the National Curriculum*. London: HMSO.

Gardner, P. (1994) Representations of the relationship between science and technology in the curriculum. *Studies in Science Education*, 24(1): 1–28.

Goldsworthy, A., Watson, R. and Wood-Robinson, V. (2000) *Developing Understanding in Scientific Enquiry* (AKSIS Project). Hatfield: ASE.

Inkpen, M. (1992) *Penguin Small*. London: Hodder Children's Books.

Lawrence, L. and Lunt, J. (2011) Making effective links for learning. *Primary Science*, 118 (May–June 2011): 5–8.

QCDA (2010) *The National Curriculum Primary Handbook*. Coventry: QCDA (no longer in print). Available at https://orderline.education.gov.uk/gempdf/184962383X.PDF [accessed 14 Apr 2012].

Turner, J., Keogh, B., Naylor, S. and Lawrence, L. (2011) *It's Not Fair – Or Is It? A Guide to Developing Children's Ideas Through Primary Science Enquiry*. Sandbach: Millgate House and Hatfield: ASE.

Websites

Design and Technology Association website: http://www.data.org.uk – D&T resources are available, and the linked primary D&T site, although many are accessible only to members.

PrimaryUpdate: http://www.primaryupd8.org.uk.

Ricky Explores Antarctica: http://antarcticapuppet.primaryblogger.co.uk/ [accessed 21 Apr 2012].

10 Planning for cross-curricular learning

Di Stead

Introduction

Planning is an essential part of the teaching and learning cycle if teachers are to provide children with a relevant, broad and balanced curriculum. The commitment to rigorous planning at all levels in the school when introducing a cross-curricular approach to curriculum planning is high-lighted in this chapter. It will be apparent from the case study outlined later in the chapter that the vision and leadership from the headteacher was crucial for the successful development of their curriculum. The sup-port of the senior management to motivate staff on the journey was essen-tial to give teachers the confidence and the opportunities to put all their ideas into practice, to take risks and try out new ideas. However, we argue that care should be taken to avoid repeating mistakes from the past when links between subjects could be tenuous.

This chapter explores how to approach planning cross-curricular work when science is the lead subject in the topic – which Laurie (2011: 132) advocates as an effective strategy when planning 'rigorous' cross-curricular teaching and learning.

To integrate or separate?

Comments made in review papers on the National Curriculum (DfE, 2011) indicated that teachers and schools would welcome an opportunity to explore cross-curricular ways of working. However, an important message in the previous chapters is that cross-curricular work is just one approach to teaching and learning, and the first decision should be *when to use* cross-curricular study. This decision, *when* to adopt single-subject teaching and *when* to adopt a more cross-curricular approach, has to be made by individual schools. The Cambridge Review points out that:

> Schools need to think carefully about which aspects might be taught separately and which combined, which need to preserve disciplinary integrity and which are amenable to thematic treatment.

(Alexander, 2009: 55)

The Rose Review (Rose, 2009: para 2.37) also advocated cross-curricular studies as part of the whole curriculum, because they provide opportunities to develop good attitudes and dispositions to learning. It argued that a combination of discrete subject teaching and cross-curricular studies enable children to develop an understanding of both what to study and how to study. Furthermore, Hayes (2010), in a critique of cross-curricular teaching and learning, points out that advocates of this approach argue that an emphasis on discrete subject teaching creates artificial barriers in younger children's minds and consequently they fail to make a secure connection between different areas of knowledge. On the other hand, children gain a holistic view of learning when the curriculum is taught as an integrated whole.

Task 10.1 Integrate or separate?

Both Alexander (2009: 55) and Rose recommend that schools should decide 'when learning is best served by teaching subject content discretely and systematically', but give 'children ample opportunities to use and apply their developing subject knowledge, skills and understanding in cross-curricular studies' (DCSF, 2008: 2009).

The decision about what science is best taught discretely and what can be linked effectively to other subjects should be made at the long-term planning stage.

Are there any science topics which you think should be taught discretely? What are these? Why do you think they should be taught discretely?

Principles for planning cross-curricular work

Decisions about how to implement any curriculum start at the school level. At the heart is the school's philosophy about how children learn and, for the science curriculum, what makes good science teaching. The 'goals for pupil learning need to originate in the shared values and goals of the school and wider community' (Harlen and Qualter, 2009: 282).

In Chapter 1 we pointed out that both science education and a cross-curricular approach to teaching and learning are informed by the constructivist view of learning. Consequently any planning at school level should to take into consideration three key features of constructivism:

1   Children make sense of the world they live in (Allen, 2010). Children examine what they see 'with their own eyes' in the light of what they already know, including making links across subjects. However, unless the links between activities are made explicit by a knowledgeable other, the connections children may make can lead to alternative conceptions about how the world works. In addition, teachers should acknowledge that children have well formed ideas before they enter their classrooms, and should be given help to recognize what they already know so they can begin to link new ideas to their existing ideas. Furthermore, children learn more effectively when teachers make the links between subjects explicit (Loughran, 2010: 91–103).

2   The role of practical working in constructivism. Parker (2004: 22) highlights the importance of providing a rich learning environment, with plenty of opportunities for children to be involved with investigative, practical work, to enable children to construct and reconstruct meaning, particularly in science.

3   Telling children 'the correct answer' will not necessarily change their ideas. They need to be personally involved with constructing meaning. If they are interested and the focus of the lesson is relevant to them they are more likely to become engaged. This is supported by a report for the Chemical Industry Education Centre by Porter and Parvin (2008), which stated that children learn science best when their learning is set in an everyday situation. They suggest that using real life contexts and making school science relevant and engaging is important. A cross-curricular approach can often provide an interesting context for children's learning, set in everyday life.

When planning for effective links between subjects it is important that teachers take note of the distinctive features of both science and the other subject so that the integrity of each subject is preserved. As Savage (2011: 40) points out, there are concepts, knowledge and skills inherent to each subject. Some questions that should be considered are:

- How clear are you of the differences in skills between the subjects?
- What do we mean when we say that children will investigate?

- Do we use the same approach when we investigate in science as when we investigate in history or geography or art?
- Are the questions we ask in science the same as they are in history or geography or art?
- Do we collect data in a different way?

If we accept that making effective links between science and other subjects can enhance science learning, we need to think about how to make these links. Czerniak (2007) describes several different models for planning cross-curricular study:

1   A content-specific approach when similar content is taught in both science and another subject. For example, children learn about water in both geography and science; in both art and science children learn about properties of materials and about changes to materials. This approach is used when children apply their science knowledge in another subject, for example using their knowledge of electrical circuits to design and make a toy electric car.

2   A process approach when similar skills and processes are taught. For example, collecting and analysing data for a science investigation provides a context for learning about data-handling in mathematics, for instance when learning how temperature affects the rate at which substances melt. Observation is a key skill for both scientists and artists, and an art lesson looking at the work of an artist such as Georgia O'Keefe can provide a context for looking at the structure of a flower, looking at similarities and differences between different flowers.

3   A methodological approach when subjects have similar ways of working. For example both science and history use investigative approaches. Both scientists and historians make a hypothesis; collect, analyze and evaluate data; classify; and consider the validity of the evidence (Brodie and Thompson, 2009).

A further model for planning a cross-curricular study is a thematic approach, where a limited number of discrete subjects contribute to children's learning on a chosen theme. For example, when learning about the Second World War, children can investigate which material makes the most effective blackout; they could also look at the effect of rationing on diet and consider how a healthy diet was maintained.

Ensuring coherence and continuity in children's learning across the school is important (Harlen and Qualter, 2006: 235). The science subject leader has an important contribution to make in planning and monitoring cross-curricular teaching to ensure that the National Curriculum for science is covered and to consider progression. Planning for progression has never been easy, but planning in a cross-curricular way presents teachers with even more challenges. How can a school ensure there is planned progression in skills at the same time as progression in ideas? Is the progression in a skill practised/developed in science matched by the progression of the same skill in the subject which is enhancing the science learning? A whole-school approach, as illustrated in the Hursthead Junior School case study, is necessary alongside a clear understanding by individual teachers of the progression of both scientific skills and skills in the other focus subject. For example, Table 6.2 in the history chapter teased out the progression in history skills using the National Curriculum level descriptors (Rowley and Cooper, 2009). Information about the progression in individual science skills, with examples to illustrate the levels, is clearly presented in *Making Sense of Primary Science Investigations* (Goldsworthy and Feasey, 1994). A more recent book which supports planning for progression in science enquiry skills is *It's Not Fair – Or Is It?* (Turner et al., 2011), which has a series of useful skills progression grids outlining progression from Reception to later primary.

A further role for the subject leader is to support staff, acting as advisor, supporter and collaborator (Harlen and Qualter, 2009: 312). Ofsted (2008) highlights the importance of joint planning which utilizes the expertise of the science subject leader, other subject leaders and the class teacher. This support may develop the confidence required for a class teacher to be responsive to their children's interests and needs. Reviewing what is taught and what is learned and evaluating the impact of the teaching is also necessary.

When planning, teachers also have a duty to ensure that any statutory requirements are met, that there is coherence across subjects, that there is an appropriate balance between subjects and that the planned teaching and learning is not superficial. Using the National Curriculum programmes of study to inform planning has been shown to be a successful strategy to support this planning (Ofsted, 2008; Jarvis, 2009). Some teachers find spider diagrams a useful tool when planning cross-curricular teaching arranged around a central topic or theme. Others find mind mapping (Buzan, 2003) a useful technique for organizing their thinking and as a quick way of seeing the links made between ideas. Another approach is the diagram used in Chapter 9, Planning for 'Penguin Small' (Figure 9.2).

At the centre of good planning is the consideration of what we want our children to learn. Harlen and Qualter (2009: 157) suggest that a cross-curricular approach may require a broader focus than when planning for discrete subjects, and claim that 'clear, broadly based goals' for a lesson are essential. In shorter term planning, learning objectives for *each* subject need to be clear. Teachers then select or design activities which they consider best teach the intended learning. This selection of how best to teach what we want the children to learn is particularly important when activities may teach science *and* another subject. To maintain the integrity of the subjects under study and to 'avoid compromising subjects in efforts to *"fit them"* to a theme', Barnes (2011: 199–213) recommends limiting to three or four the number of subjects which contribute to a cross-curricular theme or study.

It is good practice when planning for cross-curricular work to give children a role in the planning. A study by Ofsted (2010: para 38) into creative approaches to teaching and learning found that when children were more involved with planning they had 'the sense of individual discovery rather than of seeing themselves shepherded along a path that had already been mapped out for them'. They also found that 'pupils with widely differing abilities and interests were fully engaged and appropriately challenged' (para 37). This supports the argument that cross-curricular work fosters a child-led approach and that an advantage is that activities or topics can be changed or adapted in response to the interests of the children or to current events. For this to be effective, teachers need the freedom and confidence to be flexible in their approach to planning. However, to avoid planning becoming too onerous such changes should not be too frequent. In addition, if planning is done in haste the links made between subjects could become superficial.

To sum up, schools should take a measured approach to developing cross-curricular work. Laurie (2011: 127) suggests that successful planning for effective teaching and learning should include:

- Coherence in learning between different subjects.
- Making learning more relevant.
- Building and reinforcing key concepts and skills.
- Providing contexts for using and applying subject-specific skills and concepts.

Case study: One school's experience of adopting a cross-curricular approach

Hursthead Junior School is a three form entry junior school in a leafy suburb of Stockport, although the catchment is from a wide socio-economic group. In this case study the headteacher explains how she set about introducing a cross-curricular approach, and the challenges the school faced.

The story started seven or eight years ago. Although a high-achieving school, the staff at Hursthead Junior School did not want to sit back and become a coasting school. Reflecting on the needs of the children as high achievers on entry, they were concerned to accelerate the children's learning and wanted to drive the curriculum forward and make it challenging. The headteacher thought that using a cross-curricular approach to teach creatively could help; however she knew that it would take a number of years to develop and embed the practice. So, five years ago, supported by the publication of *Excellence and Enjoyment* (DfES, 2003) which encouraged schools 'to take control of their curriculum, and to be more innovative and to develop their own character', and with the full backing of the governing body, the school embarked on a four-year project to develop a curriculum to engage and challenge their children.

To try out this approach the school started with themed days – for example designing experiments to test biscuits, including dunking biscuits; and themed weeks across the school such as 'Titanic Week' and 'Maggot Week', where children planned investigations, and 'Vegetable Week', which involved working in the school kitchen. Wherever possible the learning was driven by the children.

This themed teaching had an immediate impact both on pupil enjoyment and the quality of learning. Through work scrutiny, display, assemblies and parents' responses the school noticed an improvement in the quality of the children's work and the children's enjoyment. They gathered evidence to show progression across the school.

Based on this experience, the headteacher felt that the school had to take the initiative and begin developing their own curriculum. She felt they could not wait for a prescriptive curriculum imposed by government. She acknowledged that they had to be brave but also that a safety net was needed in case the project did not work out as she hoped. This was done by keeping English and mathematics as discrete subjects until links became obvious, but ICT was embedded throughout. She felt this would help to reassure Ofsted, visitors, parents and definitely experienced teachers that the National Curriculum was being followed.

Figure 10.1 shows the five-year action plan for introducing the cross-curricular approach at Hursthead Junior School.

Year one: exploration

The senior leadership team (SLT) visited other schools to see the creative curriculum in action, including where International Primary Curriculum (IPC) (http://www.greatlearning.com/ipc) and Creative Learning Journey

Year 1	Year 2	Year 3	Year 4 NOW	Year 5
S.D.P. • Research papers • National picture • Investigate good practice • Visit schools • Family of Schools • Attend training • NCSL • Develop themed week trials and feedback • Costs	S.D.P. • SLT visit schools and observe good practice • Consult with outside agencies • Present to SLT • SLT create planning format • Present to governors • Present to teachers for trial • Plan first theme • Deliver first theme and evaluate with broad group assessment quality of teaching/activities/pupil enjoyment in Summer term • Costs	S.D.P. • As year progresses develop 5 more areas of learning • Commit inservice days, staff meetings and PPA time • Provide subject manager non contact time • Subject manager reports required • Liaise with Key Stage One • Costs	S.D.P • Review and monitor quality of activities • Refine assessment to include specific groups and individuals • Teachers move year groups to have overview of progression in Key Stage. • Identify gaps in coverage • Provide opportunities to teach some areas discreetly if not appropriate to theme • Lesson observation • Costs	S.D.P. • Review and monitor quality of teaching and pupil enjoyment • Analyse impact of themes on SATs results • Focus on activities to support identified groups • Be prepared to adjust planning to new National Curriculum requirements • Monitor progression of skills and knowledge • Monitor time management and effectiveness of planning • Costs

Figure 10.1 Hursthead Junior School's five-year action plan

(http://www.thecreativelearningjourney.co.uk) had been introduced. The school chose to visit contextually similar schools from the Greater Manchester Family of schools. Of course nothing proved to be a perfect fit and consequently they decided to develop their own curriculum. Although she knew that it would be a huge amount of work, the headteacher felt that the staff had the expertise to develop and deliver a creative curriculum without relying on published materials. Despite substantial costs allocated to providing planning time, it would be more effective because teacher learning takes place through discussion and sharing practices (Simon et al., 2011).

She was also aware that they would need to look carefully to see how best to facilitate transition from Key Stage 1 to 2 and into secondary school.

Year two: writing, trialling

This year INSET days and staff meetings were allocated to developing themed planning. One theme lasting four to six weeks per year group was developed, to take place in the second half of the summer term. To scaffold the staff planning, the headteacher, deputy headteacher and science subject leader provided a structure and simple proformas. The teachers in each year group took ownership of the detailed planning and designed the activities to achieve the learning intentions, taking note of the National Curriculum requirements. The assessment of these objectives was an essential part of the planning. When planning the themes the teachers were expected, when appropriate, to make explicit links to English, mathematics and ICT in each unit.

During the year it became clear that the staff were on board as they noticed the high quality of outcomes for pupils from this approach to teaching. In lesson observations the SLT had evidence of good practice where teachers provided excellent feedback to children and indicated their next steps for learning. Staff saw that the senior leadership team valued their efforts.

Year three: developing new materials

The headteacher wanted progress to be consistent and measured, while wanting to ensure that staff had quality time to plan. It was important this year that teachers were able to build on the work they had done in the previous year. To ensure consolidation, the teachers stayed in the same year as they had taught the previous year, but were expected to develop a further five topics (Table 10.1). To this end the headteacher ensured that there was designated revenue to release staff. Staff recognized

Table 10.1 Hursthead's creative curriculum overview

	Year 3	Year 4	Year 5	Year 6
Autumn 1	I want my Mummy!	Who do you think you are?	Final frontier	New beginnings
Autumn 2	Puppet theatre	Bright sparks	Fragile Earth	Life cycles
Spring 1	What a load of rubbish!	Indian inspirations	Communication – is there anybody out there?	Where do we live?
Spring 2	The Olympic Games	Chocolate	Conflict	Shelters
Summer 1	Food, glorious food!	Survival	Extreme factor deserts and rainforests	Inventions
Summer 2	Exploring caves	The deep, blue sea	Food and farming	The world of sport

that to ensure coverage of the science National Curriculum there was sometimes a need for two or three discrete science lessons per week. A further development this year was the expectation that each themed area began with an educational visit or activity day in school to kick-start the topic. A highlight towards the end of the topic 'What a load of rubbish!' was the 'Trashion Show' (Table 10.2).

Year four: building and consolidating

Again, quality of learning was centre stage. Now that there was a skeleton plan in place, the role of the subject coordinator became more important. They had taken ownership of their subjects, through developing policy and requisition of resources for example, which has been good for their professional development. They were responsible for monitoring progress by collecting measurable data as well as producing evidence banks. Samples of work from Year 3 to Year 6 were collected to check progression of skills and knowledge. A range of assessment tools were used to measure impact, including anecdotal evidence, such as listening to the pupil voice, and more formal methods, for example surveying attitudes.

As part of the monitoring of science, the school decided to compare the children's attainment with that of previous years. At this point, the government had abandoned testing for science. The children sat an old science SATs paper for which the school had the reported results. The results showed that 90 per cent of children achieved level 4 or above, whereas 99 to 100 per cent level 4 had been achieved before this project began. The school was not discouraged by this apparent dip in the attainment because they had evidence that the quality of children's learning had improved. The children enjoyed learning science and demonstrated that they knew how to enquire, and showed a determination in their investigations. It could be argued that testing using SATs papers measured knowledge while the new approach to teaching focused on science skills. At the end of the fourth year the school continues to believe in this approach and is very confident in what they are doing because they have evidence of quality learning.

Final year: review

At the time of writing, the headteacher talked about what was planned for the final year of this project. The school intended to look closely at the progress and attainment of specific groups of children, for example children with English as an additional language, quiet high-achieving girls and ethnic groups.

Table 10.2 Hursthead's timetable for 'What a load of rubbish!'
What a load of rubbish! Year 3 Spring Term 1

	Week 1	Week 2	Week 3	Week 4	Week 5	Week 6
Monday	Unit 1 – GEOGRAPHY: Can I explain what rubbish is?	Unit 3 – GEOGRAPHY: Can I explain how waste is disposed of?	Unit 5 – GEOGRAPHY: Can I explain what the '3 Rs' stand for?	Unit 6 – HISTORY: Can I explore how people learned to reuse food during WW2?	Unit 8 – GEOGRAPHY: Can I explore why we need to reduce the number of plastic bags?	Unit 10 – GEOGRAPHY: Can I identify developing countries on a map of the world?
Tuesday	Unit 2 – GEOGRAPHY: Can I explore whether packaging on food is always essential?	Unit 4 – GEOGRAPHY: Can I discuss some of the problems of disposing of rubbish in landfill sites?	Unit 7A – GEOGRAPHY: Can I create an outfit reusing materials from around the home?	Unit 7B – GEOGRAPHY: Can I create an outfit reusing materials from around the home? TRASHION SHOW	Unit 9A – GEOGRAPHY: Can I explain what can be made from rubbish?	Unit 11A – GEOGRAPHY: Can I discover how developing countries tackle recycling?
Wednesday	Unit 1 – SCIENCE: Can I classify different types of materials accurately?		Unit 2 – SCIENCE: Can I explain why some materials are suitable for making a particular object?	Unit 3 – SCIENCE: Can I test the strength of carrier bags?	Unit 4 – SCIENCE: Can I test the absorbency of paper towels?	Unit 5 – SCIENCE: Can I choose the best material to make an umbrella?
Friday	Unit 1A – ART: Can I respond imaginatively to the story of Frog Belly Ratbone?	Unit 1B – ART: Can I respond imaginatively to the story of Frog Belly Ratbone?	Unit 2A – ART: Can I create a weaving from recycled materials?	Unit 2B – ART: Can I create a weaving from recycled materials?	Unit 9B – GEOGRAPHY: Can I explain what can be made from rubbish?	Unit 11B – GEOGRAPHY: Can I discover how developing countries tackle recycling?

Looking to the future

The headteacher recognized the investment of time and creativity made by the staff over the previous four years. However, to continue their development the school would now review and modify their curriculum and practice, where necessary.

To develop the expertise of the staff, the school had traditionally moved teachers to different age groups every couple of years. This practice was briefly suspended to allow staff to use their energy to plan and consolidate their cross-curricular practice. To enable staff to acquire an overview of the curriculum and monitor continuity and progression, senior management planned to reintroduce the practice of moving staff between age groups. This could facilitate a dialogue of when is the best time to teach a specific piece of knowledge or a skill, and is acknowledged as good practice in developing expertise (Loughran, 2010).

The headteacher was aware that the school would have to respond to future government initiatives. However the skills developed throughout the last few years, such as monitoring and the ability to come to shared understandings, gives them confidence that they will be able to respond positively and flexibly to new directives. She acknowledged that any change has implications for budgeting.

On reflection, the headteacher recognized that committing the school to a cross-curricular approach was a leap of faith but right for their school and all its pupils. The key to success was convincing the staff of this approach, perhaps because they saw that the impact on pupils' learning was immense. She praised the commitment and dedication of her staff, who have worked tremendously hard to ensure that the curriculum flourished.

Although recognizing that a cross-curricular approach might not suit every school, the headteacher would give this advice to someone considering embarking on the same journey.

As a headteacher:

- Ask yourself the question, 'What will I do if this does not progress as I expected?' Ensure that this is fully discussed with all stakeholders, including an alternative route.
- Ensure that all decisions are grounded in the school's vision and principles.
- Maintain an overview of the whole journey – the five-year plan.
- Reassure governors that you are aware of the national picture.
- Hook people in: staff, governors and parents.

- Give the staff permission to be creative and have fun while impressing on them the need to keep planning manageable and effective.

As a member of the school community:

- Consider the needs of all your children.
- Review the present curriculum with staff to see if it meets the needs of all the children.
- Start small: for example we started with one day once or twice a term, then moved to three-day projects.
- Keep parents informed at every stage.
- Decide how to respond to global events and current affairs in your teaching.
- Ensure social, moral and cultural aspects of the curriculum permeate throughout the whole school and support subject areas.
- Cultivate the pupil voice, so that children can talk positively and knowledgeably about their learning.
- Celebrate achievements with different audiences. Show children enjoying their learning. Collect a bank of evidence to support your successes. Collect samples of work, photographs.

Task 10.2

A planning tool for making cross-curricular links explicit (Table 10.3) has been devised to help identify authentic links and focus on the expected outcomes for a cross-curricular project. A completed grid for 'bread' (Table 6.1) can be found in Chapter 6.

If *Toys* was the focus of a cross-curricular topic, which other subject might you link to science? What will be the science focus, as this will influence the choice of the subject you decide to link with? For example, if you choose to teach forces through the topic *Toys*, links would not easily be developed with history. On the other hand, if you think of the materials toys are made from today and in the past then effective links with history are more likely to be made.

Use the planning tool in Table 10.3 to help check that you have made authentic links between subjects.

Table 10.3 Planning tool for making cross-curricular links explicit

TOPIC:

How does the subject provide:	Science	Other subject:
An interesting starting point or context for learning?	Think about: Visits out of the classroom and visitors to the classroom Everyday contexts Problems to solve and people to help	
Opportunities to practise skills? Use this list to help you plan the specific links between science and history: • Asking questions • Collecting evidence • Manipulating evidence • Classifying • Observations • Similarities and differences • Looking critically at the evidence • Drawing conclusions • Validity of evidence	There may be fewer links here if the focus is on knowledge	
Opportunities to develop the children's subject knowledge?	If the focus of the theme is skills then this section may be empty	

Opportunities to communicate their ideas?

Reading Chapters 2 to 8 will provide you with ideas here

Consider talk, discussing and questioning, writing for different audiences, use of a video camera and a digital microscope, databases and graph plotting, drawing

As a class teacher, when planning cross-curricular work:

- Check that your own subject knowledge is secure, to ensure that you don't underplay ideas that you do not feel confident to teach.
- Identify the links that you will make at the planning stage. Limit these to three or four subjects. Check that the links are authentic.
- Check that the planned science activities teach science and are practical in nature. Remember children learn science when they handle materials and observe what happens and then try and explain what they see. There is also a distinct body of knowledge which is known as science.
- Make links between activities and subjects explicit to help children construct meaning.
- Remember that learning is not just about transmitting knowledge but is also concerned with developing concepts.
- Ensure that the learning objectives are clear and focused, and spell out the subject area to be taught. Identify the learning *that* (propositional knowledge) and learning *how to* (practical knowledge).
- If you have planned a similar skill in two different subjects, check that you know of any differences.
- Have clear assessment criteria for each subject. Know which assessment opportunities enable you to assess which subjects. This is discussed in more detail in Chapter 11.

As a science subject leader, when you are:

1 *Supporting planning:*
   - Check that the planned activities teach science.
   - Check that the statutory requirements for the National Curriculum are met.
2 *Monitoring:*
   - Check that the links are authentic and not superficial.
   - Check that the longer term planning is progressive.
   - Check there is evidence that children make connections between areas of learning.
3 *Supporting staff:*
   - Work towards helping all staff with their own subject knowledge, both subject-specific background knowledge and pedagogical knowledge.
   - Work towards helping all staff know the progression of science skills.
   - Help develop teachers' confidence so that they can be flexible and responsive to the children's ideas.

Conclusion

For those wishing to embark on using cross-curricular approaches, or for those who have already started, careful consideration of planning by the whole school is central, as demonstrated in the case study of Hursthead Junior School. The school can ensure that depth and rigour and the integrity of the subjects is not sacrificed through thorough, but creative planning and careful monitoring and review.

References

Alexander, R. (2009) *Towards a New Curriculum: Cambridge Primary Review Interim Report.* Part 2: The Future. Cambridge: University of Cambridge.

Allen, M. (2010) *Misconceptions in Primary Science.* Maidenhead: Oxford University Press.

Barnes, J. (2011) *Cross-Curricular Learning 3–14.* Second edition. London: Sage.

Brodie, E. and Thompson, M. (2009) Double crossed: cross-curricular teaching of science and history. *School Science Review,* 90(332): 47–52.

Buzan, T. (2003) *Mind Maps for Kids.* London: Thorsons.

Czerniak, C.M. (2007) Interdisciplinary science teaching, in S.K. Abell and N.G. Lederman (eds.), *Handbook of Research on Science Education.* Mahwah, NJ: Lawrence Erlbaum Associates: 537–59.

DCSF (2008) *The Independent Review of the Primary Curriculum Interim Report.* London: DCSF.

DCSF (2009) *The Independent Review of the Primary Curriculum Final Report.* London: DCSF.

DfE (2011) *The Framework for the National Curriculum: A Report by the Expert Panel for the National Curriculum Review.* London: Department for Education.

DfES (2003) *Excellence and Enjoyment: A Strategy for Primary Schools.* London: DfES. Available at: http://webarchive.nationalarchives.gov .uk/20110202093118/http:/nationalstrategies.standards.dcsf.gov.uk/ node/85287 [accessed 29 May 2012].

Goldsworthy, A. and Feasey, R. (1994) *Making Sense of Primary Science Investigations.* Hatfield: ASE.

Harlen, W. and Qualter, A. (2006) *The Teaching of Science in Primary Schools.* Fourth edition. London: David Fulton Publishers.

Harlen, W. and Qualter, A. (2009) *The Teaching of Science in Primary Schools.* Fifth edition. London: David Fulton.

Hayes, D. (2010) The seductive charms of a cross-curricular approach. *Education 3–13: International Journal of Primary, Elementary and Early Years Education*, 38(4): 381–7.

Jarvis, T. (2009) Promoting creative science cross-curricular work through an in-service programme. *School Science Review*, 90(332): 39–46.

Laurie, J. (2011) Curriculum planning and preparation for cross-curricular teaching, in T. Kerry (ed.) *Cross-curricular Teaching in the Primary School*. London: Routledge: 125–41.

Loughran, J. (2010) *What Expert Teachers Do: Enhancing Professional Knowledge for Classroom Practice*. Abingdon: Routledge.

Ofsted (2008) *Curriculum Innovation in Schools*. London: Ofsted. Available at http://www.ofsted.gov.uk/resources/curriculum-innovation-schools [accessed 29 May 2012].

Ofsted (2010) *Learning: Creative Approaches that Raise Standards*. Manchester: Ofsted. Available at http://www.ofsted.gov.uk/publications/080266 [accessed 29 May 2012].

Parker, J. (2004) Knowledge and understanding, in J. Sharp (ed.) *Developing Primary Science*. Exeter: Learning Matters: 19–32.

Porter, C. and Parvin, J. (2008) *Learning to Love Science: Harnessing Children's Scientific Imagination*. York: CIEC, University of York. Available at: http://www.ciec.org.uk/resources/ses_report.pdf [accessed 29 May 2012].

Rose, J. (2009) *Independent Review of the Primary Curriculum: Final Report*. London: DCSF. Available at https://www.education.gov.uk/publications/standard/publicationDetail/Page1/DCSF-00499-2009 [accessed 14 Feb 2012].

Rowley, R. and Cooper, H. (2009) *Cross-curricular Approaches to Teaching and Learning*. London: Sage.

Savage, J. (2011) *Cross-curricular Learning in the Secondary School*. London: Routledge.

Simon, S., Campbell, S., Johnson, S. and Styliandou, F. (2011) Characteristics of effective professional development for early career science teachers. *Research in Science and Technological Education*, 29(1): 5–23.

Turner, J., Keogh, B., Naylor, S. and Lawrence, L. (2011) *It's Not Fair – Or Is It? A Guide to Developing Children's Ideas Through Primary Science Enquiry*. Sandbach: Millgate House and Hatfield: ASE.

11 Enhancing primary science – developing expertise

Lois Kelly

In this chapter we will discuss two cross-curricular science projects inspired by the Science, Art and Writing (SAW™) project developed by Anne Osbourn, a researcher at the John Innes Centre in Norwich. These projects were presented to teachers at Association for Science Education (ASE) science conferences, and to both PGCE and BA (QTS) student teachers in their university studies, to develop their expertise in using cross-curricular teaching and learning to enhance science. We will hear from the students and primary school children who took part in the projects. The science topics chosen as the focus for these projects were 'yeast' and 'rocks', parts of the National Curriculum that teachers tend to find difficult to teach.

How do we develop expertise?

Whenever there is a change, either in what we teach or how we teach, we embark on a journey to develop our expertise to adapt to that change. Anyone placed in a novel situation becomes a novice who needs to develop the knowledge and understanding that will help them to become more expert. Alexander (2003) argues that the journey from novice to expert is developmental, and that there are systematic changes in thinking at different stages on that journey. At the start of the journey the novice needs to become accustomed to a particular way of working and their knowledge of the subject will be limited or fragmented. As they become more competent, their knowledge and understanding becomes more cohesive and principled, and as expertise develops they become well versed in problems associated with an aspect of learning, pose questions and institute investigations that push the boundaries. Loughran (2010: 37) suggests that the difference between experts and novices is that experts make connections between the different aspects of teaching and consider the impact on their practice, while novices are less likely to make such connections, tending to view events and experiences as distinct and separate; their planning too tends to be less well organized.

The case study from Hursthead Junior School in Chapter 10 illustrates this notion that developing expertise is a process. The school staff started their development by participating in single days devoted to cross-curricular work in the first year, but by the fourth year they had developed the confidence and expertise to plan for cross-curricular themes for each half-term. It was also clear that the teachers in the school developed their expertise by working collaboratively, sharing and discussing their ideas. Simon et al. (2011: 8) point out that 'many initiatives to enhance professional development are school-based' and that 'teacher learning takes place through practices that are shared, discussed and evolved collaboratively within the school structure'. At this point it is sensible to think about who might be considered to be a novice. Is it only student teachers and newly qualified teachers who are novices? Might there be occasions when a more experienced teacher could be considered to be a novice? As we noted in Chapter 1, many of the newer entrants to the teaching profession have limited experience of cross-curricular work in their own education and consequently are novices when planning effective links between subjects. If the development of expertise is envisioned as a journey, or a continuum, then another consideration is to decide where you envisage yourself, both as an individual and as an institution, on the journey to develop effective cross-curricular links which enhance primary science.

Developing expertise in making effective links between science and other subjects

Throughout this book you have been given some expert advice for making effective links between science and another subject. The purpose of this section is to consider how to develop expertise in linking subjects. As has been mentioned in previous chapters, both science education and cross-curricular approaches to teaching and learning are informed by a constructivist view of learning, and a feature of constructivism is that effective learning occurs when children make links between new ideas and their own past learning and/or their lived experiences. However, as we pointed out in Chapter 10 on planning, unless these links are made explicit the links children make can lead to an alternative idea or having unrelated ideas.

Task 11.1

Look back at the statements the children made about day and night in Task 7.3 in Chapter 7.
How have the children linked different ideas together?

Both Claxton (2002: 27) and Loughran (2010: 91–5) note that making links is a feature of 'good learners'. Claxton suggests that 'seeing how things fit together', not only in terms of their learning about a particular topic but also their personal lives, is intrinsically rewarding. It can lead to children gaining a different perspective on the world as they discover the relevance of their learning to their lives. Loughran (2010: 91–5) points out the importance of talking about making meaningful links because links which may be obvious to experts are not always obvious to the learner. Talking explicitly about making links helps learners to see that learning is interconnected and 'not a series of unrelated episodes' (Loughran, 2010: 93), which is one of the features of cross-curricular teaching and learning. It follows therefore that if teachers are to encourage learners to actively seek those links, they need to develop their expertise in planning for effective links.

Loughran (2010: 44) suggests that teachers develop their expertise by talking about activities that work in the classroom. The importance of talking explicitly to novices about linking is highlighted by this comment made by a PGCE student after working on the 'yeast' project:

I hadn't considered linking science with English and art. However, now I can identify a lot of scope for that in the future. Having discrete input for each subject gave us more of a focus for what each subject can contribute to the topic.

The next development for this novice teacher would appear to be the ability to independently analyse the robust links available between and within subject areas.

The study of microorganisms is a relatively minor part of the science curriculum in primary schools and tends to focus on investigating factors that affect the growth of microorganisms, for example investigating mould growing on bread or the fermentation of yeast. Looking through a number of primary science books written for intending teachers, very little is written about microorganisms. It is not surprising then that this is a science topic that some teachers find hard to teach. The yeast project introduced students to the 'hidden world' of microorganisms by showing them a selection of images of yeast cells. A useful resource for finding good-quality science images is the Science Photo Library (http://www.sciencephoto.com/images). This project focused on making observations to develop children's knowledge and understanding of yeast. Observation is more than simply looking at or seeing an object; it requires the person who is looking to pay attention to details such as colour, texture, odours and sounds. Claxton (2002: 23) points out that scientists and poets share the ability to pay close attention to things, and we would include artists in this list. However Jackson et al. (2010) note that if children are to make high-quality observations then scaffolding is needed. In Chapter 2, on English enhancing science, Alison Brade described scaffolding PGCE students' observations of the yeast cells and the process of developing 'yeast poems'. To extend the students' observations, an art activity was then introduced. They were encouraged to discuss the line and form of the yeast cells and make simple line drawings and patterns inspired by the shapes they could see. Next each student was given a small piece of clay and asked to mould one of the yeast cells they could see in the image. A board was then passed around the class and each student added their 'yeast cell' to produce a representation of a yeast colony. Following this introduction the students then investigated the factors that affected the growth of yeast.

To develop their expertise, the students were then encouraged to talk about how the links between each subject had enhanced their learning. One student recognized that explicitly linking subjects together helps to make learning more relevant:

> This project consolidated vocabulary and scientific ideas and phenomena. It also made English quite fun and inspiring such as when we made poems about yeast. English and art were linked together and they seemed a lot more relevant. You could observe the experiment and get ideas from this about which to write.

As has already been mentioned, children become more effective learners when they develop their expertise in making links. This was explored with a group of Year 5 children who took part in the 'yeast' project. As well as recognizing what they had learned about yeast, they were able to explain the links between science and poetry. One child's comments reflected the comments of the PGCE student in relation to providing a context for developing science vocabulary – 'you learned science words to use in the poem' – while another child thought the link was 'important because scientists use words to describe things'. Although the children needed very little science-specific vocabulary to describe the yeast cells, their poems illustrate the close attention they paid to the images of yeast.

Yeast, Yeast, Yeast
Lumpy, soft, squidgy
Balloon-shaped, multi-coloured
Sandy, slim and thin
Yeast
Ruby (Year 5)

Yeast, Yeast, Yeast
Potato-shaped, lemon-shaped, golf-ball shaped too,
Multi-coloured, rainbow-coloured, close-knit,
Powdery, microscopic, millions
Yeast
Jessica, Holly, Georgia, Grace (Year 5)

Figures 11.1 and 11.2 show the children developing their artistic responses to the yeast images. Again the children were able to explain the link between science and art, as this comment shows: 'I felt like an artist when we modelled the yeast. Learning science would help an artist because otherwise you wouldn't know what you were doing.'

When developing expertise to make effective links between subjects to enhance learning and conceptual development, it is important to be aware of different models for planning cross-curricular studies because, as Hayes (2010) reminds us, this approach to planning can be interpreted in a variety of ways. This project fits the 'process approach' to cross-curricular planning (Czerniak, 2007) as observation was the link between science, English and art.

A feature of effective professional development is to identify where you are and to know the next steps. Fogarty (2009) suggests we can think of the process of developing more cross-curricular or integrated approaches to teaching and learning as a continuum. At one end the curriculum is fragmented, with subjects taught separately as distinct disciplines. As schools and teachers develop their expertise the curriculum becomes:

- Connected: topics within a discipline are connected.
- Nested: social, thinking and content skills are targeted within a subject area.
- Sequenced: similar ideas are taught in concert, although subjects are separate.
- Shared: team planning and/or teaching that involves two disciplines focuses on shared concepts, skills or attitudes, which was discussed in the case study in Chapter 10.

Figure 11.1   'Hidden worlds': observing the line and form of yeast cells

- Webbed: thematic teaching using a theme as a base for instruction in many disciplines. The 'Rubbish' topic at Hursthead Junior School is an example of this.
- Threaded: thinking skills, social skills, multiple intelligences and study skills are threaded throughout the disciplines.
- Integrated: priorities that overlap multiple disciplines are examined for common skills, concepts and attitudes. For example,

Figure 11.2   Interpreting yeast images: making a model of a yeast colony from salt dough

geographical enquiry and historical enquiry (Chapters 5 and 6) are similar to science enquiry.
- Immersed: the learner integrates by viewing all learning through the perspective of one area of interest.
- Networked: the learner directs the integration process through selection of a network of experts and resources.

While it is acknowledged that this process is not necessarily straightforward, this continuum could be useful for self-evaluation and setting targets. It is also important to consider that the level of integration possible may often be dependent on the approach or on the content of the topic.

Developing expertise to assess cross-curricular work

One of the challenges of a cross-curricular approach to teaching and learning mentioned in Chapter 1 was assessment. A question that is frequently asked about assessing cross-curricular work is 'What is the main focus of the assessment?' Talking recently with a headteacher about the focus their school had on ensuring that children's writing had a relevant context and purpose, she mentioned that one of the dilemmas that the teachers were wrestling with when assessing writing that related, for example, to the children's science work was 'Do I assess their knowledge and understanding of science or do I assess their literacy skills?' Many teachers will recognize this tension, particularly when there is a mismatch between a child's science ability and their writing skills. I am sure that, like me, you can think of children who have a good understanding of science but who are not able to communicate the full extent of this in writing. Rennie et al. (2011: 144) suggest that one of the main reasons for this dilemma, when assessing children's learning in a cross-curricular context, is that discrete subject knowledge has been 'valued as a major indicator of students' learning for so long that we lack methods and explanatory frameworks to capture and enable analysis of learning that is not strictly discipline based'. They argue for the need for a more multifaceted approach when assessing learning in a cross-curricular context that takes account of how children apply their subject knowledge when working across subject boundaries.

In answer to the question, 'How can we assess cross-curricular and creative learning?', Barnes (2011: 215–31), like Taylor (2011: 142–52), makes a strong case for using the principles of assessment for learning, where the assessment is informed by teachers' knowledge, among other things, of National Curriculum level descriptors. Good practice in assessment stems from careful planning and having clear learning objectives which inform the assessment. With careful consideration we suggest it is possible to assess children's learning from two or more different subject perspectives. We argue, like Savage (2011: 139–51), that it is the accumulation of assessment evidence from each of the subjects which provides an insight into children's learning. This will be illustrated by looking at assessment throughout a short cross-curricular project focusing on rocks.

Morris (2010) points out that when investigating rocks children need to be encouraged to look for clues that will help them investigate and solve geological puzzles. Much of this evidence can be obtained by careful observation, however children need to learn to use 'precise, descriptive language' (Morris, 2010) to describe the rocks they observe. She states the importance to geologists of knowing the precise colour of the rock, the size and shape of crystals, the size and shape of grains, for working out how and when the rocks had been formed. From this it is easy to see how both English and art can enhance children's learning about rocks. As a third year BA (QTS) student commented:

Making effective links between subjects was highlighted for me by creating a haiku. I was able to give a more descriptive analysis of the rocks using the language I had previously learned.

Sandy, grainy, rock,
Hot paprika, ginger glow,
Stopping river flow.
Rock haiku by third year BA (QTS) students

What type of rock do you think was the stimulus for this poem? What makes you think this? Where do you think the group of students were when they saw the rock? Have the students used precise language to record their observations of the rock? Is there an effective use of the haiku to develop imagery? If you were to assess this poem would you be assessing the students' poetry writing skills or their ability to make high-quality observations of rocks? Is it possible to assess both science and their poetry writing?

Now consider the following adjective poem, written by a second group of third year BA (QTS) students:

Rocks, Rocks, Rocks
Rough, grainy, hard rocks
Dull, dense, dark rocks
Sharp, shiny, shimmering rocks
Rocks

This poem, too, used students' observations of rocks as a stimulus for poetry writing. Is this poem concerned with developing an image of a particular rock? What image of rocks do you get by reading this poem? Where might the rocks have been? Has either science or English been compromised when writing the poem? How significant is this in assessing the poem?

Assessment during a cross-curricular study of rocks

A common theme running through this book is that when planning cross-curricular work teachers need to keep in mind both the integrity of the subjects which contribute to a particular study as well as helping children to make links between the different subjects. As previously mentioned, this inevitably causes tension when deciding what and how to assess. Can one activity assess more than one subject? How do teachers ensure that their assessment makes judgements about what children have learned in each subject? The activity below illustrates that teachers can provide opportunities not only to gather information about what the children know, or what they can do, or their attitude to their learning, but also demand that the children reflect on their learning. Can you use the photographs of children working as evidence that learning has taken place? Is the 'balloon' iPad app (see Figure 11.4) which allows children to annotate their photograph using a speech bubble a useful tool for assessment? Who for?

As you read through the sequence of learning, consider whether the activity is assessing more than one subject. Also consider who will benefit from the information gathered and what they will do with the information. How does the assessment help inform the next steps in the children's learning? We suggest one sequence of activities, but is there an alternative route or pathway? Would writing the poem first give children the vocabulary to use in the 'same but different' activity?

Step 1: Same but different

The children will know that differences and similarities between rocks can be observed.

Activity: The children were given a selection of eight different named rocks. The first child was invited to choose two rocks and make two statements about the rocks:

    a)   these rocks are the same because ...
    b)   these rocks are different because ...

The next child chose two rocks (they were allowed to choose two completely different rocks or one that had already been chosen and a second that had not been used) and made the two statements about this pair of rocks without repeating anything that had already been said. As the set of rocks was passed round, the children focused on the finer detail of the rocks (Figure 11.3).

Assessment: Talk with the children about how easy it was to make the pair of statements. How did their observations change as they repeated this activity? What did they begin to take more notice of? How did they respond to and build on each other's statements about similarities and differences?

Figure 11.3 The 'same but different' activity encourages children to look more carefully

Step 2: Making a rock identification key

The children will learn:

that observable features help us to separate rocks into groups
that an identification key is compiled by asking a sequence of closed questions

Activity: The children were given a set of rocks and asked to think of a question that could only have a 'yes' or 'no' answer, using characteristics which they observed and would sort the rocks into two similar-sized groups. Once the rocks had been sorted, they chose one of the two groups and asked a further question which would sort those rocks into two groups. This continued until they had completed the identification key.

Assessment: Talk with the children about what they looked for to help them group the rocks.

Talk to the children about how easy it was to ask questions which require a yes/no answer.

How many questions used scientific criteria to sort the rocks?

Did they develop a logical sequence of questions to produce an identification key?

Step 3: Writing rock poems

The children will learn:

> *to use precise, descriptive and imaginative language to describe rocks*
> *that similes develop imagery*

Activity: Each group of children chose a rock to observe in more detail and were encouraged to use hand lenses so they could pay more attention to the detail in the rock (Harlen and Qualter, 2009: 126). As described in Chapter 2, questions were used to scaffold their observations. Children wrote on sticky notes the answer to the question 'What colours can you see in your rock?' (Figure 11.4). The children were given paint charts to inspire them to describe the colours in the rock and help develop more imaginative writing. Next they were asked about the texture of the rock. Finally the children were asked to examine the structure of the rock, the

Figure 11.4 Children describing colours in granite

shape and size of the grains or crystals. As part of this exercise the children were encouraged to extend their description of the rocks by developing similes. For example granite was described as *sparkly* so the children were invited to think of phrases that would give a better image and eventually decided to use the phrase *'as sparkly as a starry night'*. The children then composed a simile poem by arranging and rearranging the similes they had written on the post-it notes. Cabrera (2008) found that poetry was an effective strategy to enhance children's science learning and language development.

Granite is
As jagged as pineapple
As rough as a rug
As sparkly as a starry night
By Dan and Lauren (Year 4)

Limestone is
As rough as sandpaper
Golden like a labrador
As crumbly as a pie
By Amelia and Theo (Year 4)

Assessment: Talk with the children about developing similes to create images for the poem. Discuss the similes they chose to include and those they decided to discard.

Talk with the children about the vocabulary used to describe the rock.

Talk with the children about the evidence they have obtained from observing rocks.

Step 4: Rock collages

The children will learn:

> *that different rocks have different patterns and textures*
> *to make a personal response using collage to represent the patterns and textures*

Activity: The earlier discussions about the texture, colours and patterns the children had observed were then explored further in an art activity. Using a variety of different papers, the children were asked to tear, fold and crumple pieces of paper to make a collage which created an impression, but not an accurate representation, of the rock they had been studying (Figure 11.5).

Figure 11.5 Making a collage: making a personal response to the colours and patterns in sandstone

Assessment: Talk with the children about how they made the decision to use the materials to represent the rock used as a stimulus.

Do the collages represent both visual and tactile elements of the rock?

Can the children discuss the similarities and differences between their collages?

Although gathering evidence of children's learning for the different subjects is important, there are aspects of learning that are not as easy to assess but are significant. Consider this comment made by a third year BA (QTS) student when discussing the impact on her of using a cross-curricular approach to study rocks.

This opened my eyes to how interesting learning about rocks could actually be. I had observed lessons about rocks. These were restricted to the classroom, looking at various types of rocks. In these lessons, where creativity can be very restricted, the resources are limited and children do not learn very well because the teaching is not very stimulating.

Another key factor for the student was the fact that this was 'out of classroom learning'. As a stimulus for the project, the students visited a local area of Special Scientific Interest (SSI). The impact of the change of venue on her development should not be underestimated, and the impact will often be as great, if not greater, on a child.

For me as a teacher, helping learners change their attitude to learning and fostering their interest in a particular area of study is more rewarding than assessing whether they have met a particular learning objective. A year after being introduced to this project during in-service training, one teacher commented on the change in attitude of the children in her class to studying rocks. She told me that the children had become so fascinated by rocks that she had had to stop them bringing rock samples into her class!

Task 11.2

The SAW™ project focused on English and art enhancing science. The children's responses described here raise the question of whether there are links with religious education. Many of the published schemes of work for teaching rocks and soils focus on the properties of rocks, but was this what fascinated the children in this teacher's class? Are there links with task 7.4 in Chapter 7 on RE?

Does the science here provide a suitable context to teach mathematics? Look back at Chapter 6: what would concern a geographer?

Conclusion

The success of the development of cross-curricular teaching and learning at Hursthead Junior School was accompanied by professional development for their teachers. We hope that you will have been encouraged to develop your expertise to forge effective links which enhance primary science. Assessment, vital as it is to inform about children's learning, can also help teachers reflect on what works in their classroom and their school.

We hope that you will agree with the teacher who told us that seeing a cross-curricular approach in practice had 'given me the confidence that cross-curricular approaches can enrich scientific provision rather than dilute it'.

References

Alexander, P. (2003) The development of expertise: the journey from acclimation to proficiency. *Educational Researcher*, 32(8): 10–14.

Barnes, J. (2011) *Cross-curricular Learning 3–14*. Second edition. London: Sage.

Cabrera, M. (2008) The poetry of science: the effects of using poetry in a middle school ELD science classroom. *The Electronic Journal of Literacy through Science*, 7(1): 1–42. Available at http://ejlts.ucdavis.edu/article/2008/7/3/poetry-science-effects-using-poetry-middle-school-eld-science-classroom [accessed 18 May 2012].

Claxton, G. (2002) *Building Learning Power*. Bristol: TLO.

Czerniak, C.M. (2007) Interdisciplinary science teaching, in S.K. Abell and N.G. Lederman (eds.), *Handbook of Research on Science Education*. Mahwah, NJ: Lawrence Erlbaum Associates: 537–59.

Fogarty, R. (2009) *How to Integrate the Curricula*. Third edition. Thousand Oaks, CA: Corwen.

Harlen, W. and Qualter, A. (2009) *The Teaching of Science in Primary Schools*. Fifth edition. London: David Fulton.

Hayes, D. (2010) The seductive charms of a cross-curricular approach. *Education 3–13: International Journal of Primary, Elementary and Early Years Education*, 38(4): 381–7.

Jackson, J., Dickinson, G. and Horton, D. (2010) Rocks and rhymes! A geosciences activity combining field notes and poetry. *The Science Teacher*, 77(1): 27–31.

Loughran, J. (2010) *What Expert Teachers Do: Enhancing Professional Knowledge for Classroom Practice*. Abingdon: Routledge.

Morris, K. (2010) Thinking like a geologist. *Primary Science*, 114(Sept/Oct): 30–2.

Rennie, L.J., Venville, G. and Wallace, J. (2011) Learning science in an integrated classroom: finding balance through theoretical triangulation. *Journal of Curriculum Studies*, 43(2): 139–62.

Savage, J. (2011) *Cross-Curricular Teaching in the Secondary School*. London: Routledge.

Simon, S., Campbell, S., Johnson, S. and Styliandou, F. (2011) Characteristics of effective professional development for early career science teachers. *Research in Science and Technological Education*, 29(1): 5–23.

Taylor, K. (2011) Assessing cross-curricular learning, in T. Kerry (ed.) *Cross-Curricular Teaching in the Primary School*. London: Routledge: 142–56.

Index

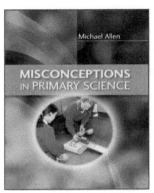

MISCONCEPTIONS IN PRIMARY SCIENCE

Michael Allen

9780335235889 (Paperback)
February 2010

This essential book offers friendly support and practical advice for dealing with the common misconceptions encountered in the primary science classroom. Most pupils will arrive at the science lesson with previously formed ideas, based on prior reasoning or experience. However these ideas are often founded on common misconceptions, which if left unexplained can continue into adulthood.

This handy book offers 100 common misconceptions and advice for teachers on how to recognise and correct such misconceptions.

Key features include:

- Examples from the entire range of QCA Scheme of Work topics for Key Stages 1 and 2
- Practical strategies to improve pupils' learning
- Support for teachers who want to improve their own scientific subject knowledge

www.openup.co.uk

 OPEN UNIVERSITY PRESS
McGraw - Hill Education

**SCIENCE BEYOND THE CLASSROOM
BOUNDARIES FOR 3-7 YEAR OLDS**

Lynne Bianchi and Rosemary Feasey

9780335241293 (Paperback)
2011

eBook also available

This innovative book aims to support schools in shifting teaching and learning in primary science by changing teacher perceptions of where science should be taught. The authors have not taken a traditional approach to the use of school grounds but a much bolder step in terms of a whole school approach to the science curriculum being taught outside.

Key features:

- Suggests practical approaches and strategies that can be used in teaching
- Offers advice on planning and types of resources to use in teaching
- Approaches that combine science and the development of personal capabilities

www.openup.co.uk

**SCIENCE BEYOND THE CLASSROOM
BOUNDARIES FOR 7-11 YEAR OLDS**

Lynne Bianchi and Rosemary Feasey

9780335241323 (Paperback)
2011

eBook also available

This innovative book aims to support schools in shifting teaching and learning in
primary science by changing teacher perceptions of where science should be
taught. The authors have not taken a traditional approach to the use of school
grounds but a much bolder step in terms of a whole school approach to the
science curriculum being taught outside.

Key features:

- Suggests practical approaches and strategies that can be used in
  teaching
- Offers advice on planning and types of resources to use in teaching
- Approaches that combine science and the development of personal
  capabilities

www.openup.co.uk

OPEN UNIVERSITY PRESS
McGraw - Hill Education

ESSENTIAL PRIMARY SCIENCE

Alan Cross and Adrian Bowden

9780335234615 (Paperback)
2009

This book offers you practical guiding principles which you can apply to every lesson. There are tips on how to ensure each lesson includes both practical and investigative elements and suggestions on how to make your lessons engaging, memorable and inclusive.

Each chapter is organized around the following structure:

- What science do you need to know and understand?
- What science do your pupils need to learn?
- What is the best way to teach these topics in the primary classroom at KS1 and KS2?

Sample pupil activities are also included and there is coverage of how to deal with common misconceptions within every chapter.

www.openup.co.uk

OPEN UNIVERSITY PRESS
McGraw - Hill Education

PRIMARY SCIENCE
Teaching the Tricky Bits

Neil Rutledge

9780335222285 (Paperback)
2010

eBook also available

The book provides a combination of engaging, practical lesson ideas and subject knowledge to help you teach the trickiest parts of primary science such as materials and their properties, magnetism, circuits, forces and life processes. The book includes a range of accessible ideas, hints and tips with a focus on providing a skills-based, problem-solving approach to learning.

Each topic area includes advice on:

- How to link the topic with other areas of learning
- Identifying and challenging common misconceptions
- How to effectively pre-assess the learners' ideas to best meet their needs
- Practical activities for challenging and developing children's ideas
- Explanatory models to help pupils consolidate their understanding

www.openup.co.uk